Tests, Testing, and
Genuine School Reform

EDUCATION
next
B O O K S

The Hoover Institution and Education Next Books gratefully acknowledge the following individuals and foundations for their support of this research on education policy and reform.

LYNDE AND HARRY BRADLEY FOUNDATION

KORET FOUNDATION

EDMUND AND JEANNIK LITTLEFIELD FOUNDATION

THE BERNARD LEE SCHWARTZ FOUNDATION, INC.

TAD AND DIANNE TAUBE
    TAUBE FAMILY FOUNDATION

THE HOOVER INSTITUTION'S KORET TASK FORCE ON K–12 EDUCATION

Tests, Testing, and Genuine School Reform

Herbert J. Walberg

HOOVER INSTITUTION PRESS

STANFORD UNIVERSITY

STANFORD, CALIFORNIA

The Hoover Institution on War, Revolution and Peace, founded at Stanford University in 1919 by Herbert Hoover, who went on to become the thirty-first president of the United States, is an interdisciplinary research center for advanced study on domestic and international affairs. The views expressed in its publications are entirely those of the authors and do not necessarily reflect the views of the staff, officers, or Board of Overseers of the Hoover Institution.

www.hoover.org

An imprint of the Hoover Institution Press

Hoover Institution Press Publication No. 610
Copyright © 2011 by the Board of Trustees of the
 Leland Stanford Junior University

First printing, 2011
18 17 16 15 14 13 12 11   9 8 7 6 5 4 3 2 1

Manufactured in the United States of America

The paper used in this publication meets the minimum requirements of the American National Standard for Information Sciences—Permanence of Paper for Printed Library Materials, ANSI Z39.48–1992.♾

Cataloging-in-Publication Data is available for the Library of Congress
ISBN-13: 978-0-8179-1354-0 (hardback : alk. paper)
ISBN-13: 978-0-8179-1356-4 (e-book)

CONTENTS

ACKNOWLEDGMENTS

My present academic appointment at Stanford University's Hoover Institution enables me, as a member of the Koret Task Force on K–12 Education, to have met twice a year with its distinguished members—John Chubb, Williamson Evers, Chester Finn, Eric Hanushek, Paul Hill, Caroline Hoxby, Tom Loveless, Terry Moe, Paul Peterson, and Russ Whitehurst. I am grateful to the task force members for their oral and written comments on previous versions of this book and to Hoover Director John Raisian and Senior Associate Director Richard Sousa for their encouragement and support. I also thank those who commented on previous versions of this book—David Anderson, George Cunningham, Noah Kippley-Ogman, Timothy Sares, John E. Stone, and Theresa Thorkildsen. Joe Bast, Oie Lian Yeh, and Trudy Wallace closely reviewed and made many useful suggestions on the penultimate version of the book. Perhaps needless to say, the opinions expressed and any remaining errors are attributable only to me since I didn't follow all the generous advice given.

1

INTRODUCTION AND OVERVIEW

The pressing need to improve achievement in American schools is widely recognized. Factors associated with high achievement are appropriate testing, along with high standards, a curriculum closely adapted to the standards, and effective teaching. Because test design and use are technical matters, legislators, state and local school board members, and educators themselves are often poorly informed about their strengths, potentials, and limitations.

Despite good intentions, responsible officials often adopt misguided testing policies, and teachers have used tests that do not accomplish their intended purposes. For these reasons, the apparent results badly inform parents, citizens, and policy-makers about the actual achievement of students—a reason for American students' mediocre performance relative to those in other economically advanced countries and relative to the new demands of the information economy.

This book draws on scientific studies of tests and their use to inform users and consumers about well-established principles of testing, current problems involving their use, and evidence-based solutions.[1] In addition, because valid tests cannot be developed without high and specific standards,

---

1. Many books concern testing, such as F. Allan Hanson's *Testing, Testing: Social Consequences of the Examined Life* (Berkeley, CA: University of California Press, 1993) and Williamson M. Evers and Herbert J. Walberg, eds., *Testing Student Learning, Evaluating Teaching Effectiveness* (Stanford, CA: Hoover Institution, 2004). The Brookings Institution, Fordham Foundation, Heartland Institute, Hoover Institution, and other organizations offer policy commentary on standardized testing.

one of the chapters discusses standards and how they should determine the plans and development of tests.

These topics are particularly important today. In the past several decades, costs of public schools have steadily and substantially risen, yet student achievement has remained stagnant. In response, schools, school districts, states, and the federal government are adapting a reform framework of "standards-assessment-accountability," with achievement tests playing a central role in assessing what students have learned.

To perform their role in the reform framework, tests must be technically adequate and well administered. They must be aligned with standards and reported accurately and fairly to the interested parties, including parents, educators, school boards, legislators, and citizens. These contributions are all the more important for high-stakes decisions such as requiring failing students to repeat grades, closing or chartering repeatedly failing schools, and paying teachers for the achievement progress of their students, topics that are also discussed in this book.

Origins of Achievement Testing

The history of testing can be traced to the beginnings of tribal societies, when they were used to determine whether young people were ready to assume adult responsibilities. The kinds of achievement tests that are the focus of this book have a far shorter history. They evolved from attempts to use scientific methods to understand human intelligence. Those investigations began with psychological interests in differences in ability, emotions, and behavior among humans. In England, for example, Sir Francis Galton surveyed the abilities of British families that led to debates about whether differences in intelligence and human functioning are attributable to heredity or environment.[2] Intelligence testing grew out of these early investigations notably in France and the U.S. around 1905, which led testing specialists to generate measures for evaluating human potential. During World War I, the United States' military used uniform tests and

---

2. Sir Francis Galton, *Hereditary Genius* (London: MacMillan Publishing, 1869). In much of education, achievement tests largely and constructively replaced intelligence testing since they indicate actual accomplishment, a more solid basis of remediation and further instruction, and prediction of further achievement in the specific area tested.

scoring for assigning personnel to jobs. By 1933, thousands of tests were in use for measuring intelligence, aptitude, and personality.[3]

After 1950 the emphasis in school testing began shifting from personality and potential to academic accomplishment or achievement in mathematics, reading, science, and other subjects and skills. By establishing common metrics for comparing achievement of individuals from all social classes, educational backgrounds, and cultures, standardized tests[4] could show objective evidence of student progress, readiness for college and graduate and professional schools, mastery of English and math, and employment skills.

College admission tests led the growth of standardized testing. The non-profit Educational Testing Service, for example, was founded in 1947 to meet the needs expressed by the American Council on Education, the Carnegie Foundation for the Advancement of Teaching, and the College Entrance Examination Board. These organizations were founded on the belief that admission policies would be more fair if students from a wide range of academic, geographical, and social backgrounds—not just descendents of alumni and Eastern Seaboard families who tended to be admitted to prestigious Ivy League schools—were given an opportunity to compete on objective, standardized tests.

Standardized tests continued to gain importance. Federal initiatives such as the Elementary and Secondary Education Act of 1965 encouraged schools to use standardized achievement tests earlier in a student's educational career to determine success in the usual school subjects. After 1970 objective examinations were used increasingly for occupational licensing and by firms to measure potential candidates' knowledge and skills. Increasingly, individuals who passed high-stakes examinations could earn diplomas, receive scholarships, and obtain licenses to practice in professional fields such as law and medicine. Failure restricted these

---

3. Gertrude H. Hildreth, *Bibliography of Mental Tests and Rating Scales* (New York: The Psychological Corporation, 1933).

4. A test is standardized if it is given under uniform conditions so that a student's resulting test score can be compared to those of other students in norm-referenced testing or a performance criterion in criterion- or standards-based testing. It is a regrettable precedent in testing that the similar terms "standard" and "standardized" are easily confused, but it can be hoped that the different meanings of these similar terms are clear in context.

opportunities, but the test results could offer individuals information on how they might correct their deficits.

Criticism of Standardized Tests

This book focuses on standardized achievement tests in which all those tested face the same tasks and conditions. High scores mean students have acquired the knowledge and skills they need to meet increasingly important standards and ready themselves for further learning in school. Most individuals take standardized tests several times during their lifetime. Necessary tasks like obtaining a driver's license require the successful completion of standardized tests, making them difficult to avoid; and tests are used routinely even in voluntary activities such as first-aid instruction.

Objections to Standardized Achievement Testing

Several influential education writers adamantly oppose current models of standardized testing and the growing emphasis on high standards and standards-based testing.[5] Alfie Kohn, for example, urges educators to "make the fight against standardized tests our top priority until we have chased this monster from our schools." Similarly, Gerald Bracey holds that "high standards and high-stakes testing are infernal machines of social destruction."

Though more tempered, several political leaders have also expressed misguided criticism about standardized achievement tests and asked policy-makers and educators to avoid them. Before he became president, for example, Sen. Barack Obama urged "innovative assessments, including digital portfolios," and making "the goal of educational testing the same as medical testing—to diagnose a student's needs,"[6] leaving out educator and student accountability for learning. This book makes clear why critics

---

5. Alfie Kohn, "Burnt at the High Stakes," *Journal of Teacher Education*, 2000, *51*, 349; Gerald Bracey, "International Comparisons: An Excuse to Avoid Meaningful Educational Reform," *Education Week*, January 23, 2002, 24.

6. Barack Obama, "Our Kids, Our Future," November 20, 2007, remarks, Manchester, New Hampshire. http://usliberals.about.com/od/education/a/ObamaEdPlan_4.htm

of standardized testing are wrong and how their views, if acted on, would undermine learning. Similarly, state legislators have allowed lax standards and ill-conceived tests to measure the progress of schools, educators, and students.

Tests as Guides to Policy

For another reason, high standards, valid tests, and accountability are important for America's future. The United States has traditionally excelled in adult accomplishments in mathematics and science as well as their practical applications, but this status is now threatened. Although top American universities are second to none in the world, the National Science Board reported that the U.S. lead is shrinking.

Foreign students, moreover, comprise an increasingly larger percentage of students in American university graduate programs in these scientific and technical fields. They often return home with the best training American universities offer. Many American students are unable to show similar levels of achievement.

Countries in Asia and Europe, moreover, have increasingly improved primary and secondary education, which may be even more decisive in scientific and technical leadership. Long before the school achievement crisis was recognized, I pointed out that the United States' welfare and prosperity benefit more from a well-educated population than from a scientific elite making scientific discoveries. Why? Credible scientific discoveries are published in peer-reviewed journals easily accessible outside the country of origin.[7] Undue efforts to discover scientific breakthroughs, moreover, can divert time and energy from making effective use of them in such fields as medicine and engineering. The United States, for example, leads the world in medical research but lags behind other countries in children's health and adult life expectancy.

The importance of high standards and attaining better test scores in schools is better recognized now than when I was writing in the early

---

7. Herbert J. Walberg, "Scientific Literacy and Economic Productivity in International Perspective," *Daedalus*, 1983, *112*, 1–28.

1980s.[8] During the past few decades, tests have been employed to measure how well K–12 students and schools have met proficiency standards. Tests and standards have become more effectively employed to advance student knowledge and skills. Analysis of K–12 standards and tests, however, reveals continuing problems.

Achievement tests today play a major role in K–12 education. They allow educators to assess the progress of students, identify their strengths and weaknesses, and plan remediation as well as revisions of teaching and curriculum. They allow parents to objectively monitor their children's learning and similarly intervene to help solve their learning problems. They enable education leaders to monitor and evaluate the progress of schools and individual teachers. Achievement tests also help citizens and legislators inform themselves about the efficiency of the large amounts of tax money spent on schools.

Surveys show that parents, citizens, and legislators strongly support tests and testing and want to see bigger consequences for excellence and failure. Educators—particularly professors in schools of education where teachers and administrators are trained—unfortunately lack testing expertise and often oppose their use. Until recently, educators prevailed. But the growing awareness that American public schools are failing to fulfill their responsibilities has changed the terms of the debate, and educators are increasingly being held accountable for disappointing achievement results.

The following chapters present much research supporting the positive and substantial effects of standardized tests. The first four chapters of this book explain the most important ideas about achievement tests and the steps in developing good tests. The reader is shown why tests are necessary, how to recognize well-made tests, and how tests are properly written. The next four chapters turn from tests to testing, that is, how tests can be best

---

8. See, for example, John Cronin, Michael Dahlin, Yun Xiang, and Donna McCahon, *The Accountability Illusion* (Washington, DC: Thomas B. Fordham Foundation, February 2009); John Cronin, Michael Dahlin, Deborah Adkins, and G. Gage Kingsbury, *The Proficiency Illusion* (Washington, DC: Thomas B. Fordham Foundation, October 2007); Chester E. Finn Jr., Liam Julian, and Michael J. Petrilli, *The State of State Standards 2006* (Washington, DC: Thomas B. Fordham Foundation, August 2006).

used. These include such topics as using tests to motivate students and teachers for better performance, how to prevent test fraud by students and teachers, and the role of tests in meeting state and national standards. In view of the continuing controversy over test design and instances of fraud, the final chapter argues that the development, administration, and scoring of tests and reporting of results should be conducted by organizations independent of traditional school authorities. A brief conclusion summarizes the key findings.

2

WHY TESTS ARE NECESSARY

Well-constructed standardized tests can help us assess how well students achieve broad, commonly valued academic goals. By evaluating the test performance of groups of students at the same grade level or who have taken the same course, and comparing it with a representative range of students from that group, it is possible to determine how well schools are fostering academic achievement.[1]

Standardized tests can measure the degree to which students attain proficiency standards for specific topics and grade levels set by state and national governments. Standardized tests also make it possible to compare students in one school system, city, state, or country to those in others systems and places, which can reveal insights on what kinds of educational practices work best and which workforce is best prepared to compete in the global economy.[2]

By designing tests with common content, directions, and scoring procedures and administering these tests under the same conditions, standardized tests facilitate reliable and valid comparisons across various groups. They make it possible to measure trends in achievement over time, identify how well student performance aligns with educational goals

---

1. Richard Cross, Theodor Rebarber, Justin Torres, and Chester E. Finn Jr., *Grading the Systems: The Guide to State Standards, Tests, and Accountability Policies* (Washington, DC: Thomas B. Fordham Foundation, January 2004).

2. William H. Schmidt, Richard Houang, and Sharif Shakrani, *International Lessons about National Standards* (Washington, DC: Thomas B. Fordham Foundation, August 2009).

or standards, and recognize gaps in who is learning and what is being learned. Increasingly, they are being used for "high-stakes" decisions such as closing repeatedly failing schools.

Physicians would be negligent in their treatment of malnourished children if they failed to regularly assess their patients' weight. Similarly, educators would be negligent if they failed to systematically assess student performance. Since American students are now tested more often, the national crisis of poor academic achievement is clearer than ever. This chapter summarizes the evidence of poor levels of achievement, what the public thinks about it, and the need for testing.

Reframing the Learning Problem

Many educators are slow to publicly acknowledge the poor achievement test results of their students and choose instead to criticize the reliability or relevance of the tests. They lobby policy-makers to ignore poor test results each year when it is time to renew public funding for schools. But policy-makers ignore poor test results at their peril.

Test information can be constructively diagnostic if used to strengthen programs. The 1998 report "A Nation Still at Risk,"[3] for example, used standardized test results to document the lack of progress in improving national math and science achievement rates in the 15 years since *A Nation at Risk* was delivered in 1983 to the U.S. secretary of education. Both reports drew attention to the poor mathematics and science achievement of American students relative to students in other economically advanced countries. Substantially higher spending and many reforms adopted since the first national report failed to raise U.S. achievement to the levels of other economically advanced countries.

More recent data shows almost no improvement in K–12 achievement rates.[4] A recent international achievement survey showed that among students in 30 countries, those in the U.S. ranked 25th in

---

3. William J. Bennett, Willard Fair, Chester E. Finn Jr., Floyd H. Flake, E.D. Hirsch Jr., Will Marshall, and Diane Ravitch, "A Nation Still at Risk," *Policy Review*, 1998, 90, 23–29; U.S. Department of Education, *A Nation at Risk: The Imperative for Educational Reform* (Washington, DC: National Commission on Excellence in Education, 1983).

4. Herbert J. Walberg, *Advancing Student Achievement* (Stanford, CA: Hoover Institution Education Next Press, 2010).

science—exceeding only Portugal, Italy, Greece, Turkey, and Mexico. American students also do poorly on tests of their English language abilities. The 2008 report prepared by the National Assessment of Educational Progress (NAEP), for example, estimated that only 24 percent of 12th-graders showed proficiency in English writing as indicated by correct spelling, proper grammar, and the skills needed to write an essay and explain complex information. Only 31 percent of 8th-graders showed proficient reading skills. Reading and other language skills, of course, are essential for further learning in all subjects and have important economic and social consequences.

Students who achieve poorly in elementary school tend to drop out of high school, and high dropout rates also confirm learning problems in the United States. After World War II, the percentages of students entering and graduating from high school in this country were the highest in the world. Today, other countries have made such rapid progress that the U.S. ranks poorly among economically advanced countries.

Between 1995 and 2005, for example, U.S. high-school completion rates dropped from 2nd to 21st place among 27 economically advanced countries, despite the U.S. having the highest per-student expenditure of all economically advanced nations. Only about 70 percent of American students graduate from high school on time, and about 1.2 million students drop out annually. Seventeen of the nation's 50 largest cities have dropout rates that are higher than 50 percent.

English, mathematics, and science skills strongly determine success in school, work, and life. Since students score so poorly in these subjects as measured on standardized achievement tests, it is understandable that parents, legislators, and citizens increasingly worry about students' and the nation's future. They are concerned about having an economy strong enough in the years ahead to pay the costs of their own Social Security and Medicare benefits—costs that Congress has obligated young people to pay.

Much evidence found in the United States and elsewhere shows how school achievement generates a wide range of benefits for individuals who score well on standardized tests. As noted by Gary Becker and Kevin Murphy, highly educated people excel in many aspects of life. "The education process itself leads people away from more harmful activities and toward better habits,"[5] including the rearing of their own children.

Parents and policy analysts are rightfully concerned about the poor performance of K–12 students and the possible consequences for this nation's economic growth. The annual loss of economic production in the United States attributable to poor quality schools was an estimated $300 billion in 2007.[6] Because we live in an information age of increasing global competition, knowledge and skill deficits will be even more damaging in the future. The outsourcing of high-skill jobs is already one consequence of American academic decline relative to other countries. Increasingly sophisticated manufacturing jobs are outsourced to Central American and East Asian countries, including China, while services such as radiological diagnosis and software development move to India.

Economic changes have discouraged many American families, but substantially higher levels of academic achievement might yield corresponding positive effects on prosperity. The Organisation for Economic Co-operation and Development has estimated that improved achievement levels could increase the present value of the U.S. economy over the next 20 years by an amount ranging from $115 trillion to $260 trillion.[7]

By assessing whether individuals are achieving the levels of academic performance needed to participate in the global economy, standardized testing can help us take the necessary measures to restore the nation's international competitiveness. A well-educated population is less likely to experience the helplessness felt by those who lack the knowledge and skills needed to participate in the global economy.

---

5. Gary S. Becker and Kevin M. Murphy, "Inequality and Opportunity," *Capital Ideas* (May 2007), 4–7. http://www.chicagobooth.edu/capideas/may07/1.aspx.

6. Eric A. Hanushek and Ludger Woessmann, *Education Quality and Economic Growth* (Washington, DC: World Bank, 2007).

7. Eric A. Hanushek and Ludger Woessmann, *The High Cost of Low Educational Performance: The Long-Run Economic Impact of Improvements in PISA Outcomes* (Paris, France: Organisation for Economic Co-operation and Development, January 2010). The figures given are in present value. The report raises questions of reverse causality and third causes as well as the question of whether the future can be projected from the past. Even so, their assumptions seem reasonable, and policy-makers and educators commonly assert the report's common-sense assumption that knowledge and skills determine at least in part the economic success of individuals and countries.

Public Support for Higher Standards and Testing

The public supports high standards and testing. Parents want to know how well their children do academically compared with other children their age and with respect to school standards. Taxpayers want to know if the money they surrender to pay for public schools is well spent to raise achievement. They would like to be assured that today's youth are sufficiently well educated to attain the prosperity that they themselves did.

Over the past four decades, more than 200 public opinion polls compiled by Richard Phelps[8] consistently show the public's strong support for standardized tests. Summarized below are several survey results. Notice the high percentage of respondents endorsing the use of standardized tests to measure educational goals and to ensure that high school graduates have acquired the knowledge and skills they need for further education and adult life.

Standardized tests should assess the following in students:	% agreement
Knowledge in core subjects	80
Ability to write a clear composition	75
Problem-solving skills	74
Academic achievement	60

Passing standardized tests for graduation should be required:	% agreement
For all students.	90
Even if your child failed the first time.	86
Even if your child does not receive a diploma.	68
Even if 20 percent of students in low-income households would not receive a diploma.	55

---

8. Richard P. Phelps, "Persistently Positive: Forty Years of Public Opinion on Standardized Testing," in Richard P. Phelps, ed., *Defending Standardized Testing* (Mahwah, NJ: Lawrence Erlbaum Associates Publishers, 2005), 1–22. To include survey results with and without the option of "undecided," reducing the results of any question to a single number, Phelps simply compared favorable and unfavorable responses.

Survey results in 2009 indicate that the public continues to favor standardized testing and the implementation of rigorous standards. Only 18 percent of the sample surveyed gave schools a grade of A or B, and this declined to 13 percent once respondents were told how the U.S. ranked among other countries on student achievement; 72 percent of the sample favored national standards and tests for all American students.[9]

In another study, when respondents were asked to identify the top priorities for 2010, 65 percent of the public named education.[10] Findings from these and other related studies offer strong evidence that the public is in favor of raising standards for American schools and using standardized tests to assess student and teacher progress.

Students' Preferences for Higher Standards and Testing

Although educators might suggest that students are intimidated or anxious about taking standardized tests, strong evidence suggests that students prefer academic rigor. Many agree with the views that schools are lax, should raise their standards, and could better hold students accountable for their performance. As revealed by national surveys, three-fourths of high school students believe stiffer examination and graduation requirements would make students pay more attention to their studies.[11] Students agree with research findings, discussed below, that suggest these accountability measures raise achievement levels.

Students want to receive credit for their academic efforts and feel their achievements would be tainted if diplomas were granted to unqualified students. In a random sample of high school students, three-fourths of the respondents said that schools should promote only individuals who master the material. Standardized tests, of course, would be necessary for objective, efficient assessments of such mastery.

---

9. William G. Howell, Paul E. Peterson, and Martin R. West, "The Persuadable Public," *Education Next*, Fall 2009, *9*, 20–29.

10. Pew Research Center, "Public's Priorities for 2010: Economy, Jobs, Terrorism," January 25, 2010. http://people-press.org/2010/01/25/publics-priorities-for-2010-economy-jobs-terrorism.

11. Ann Bradley, "Survey Reveals Teens Yearn for High Standards," *Education Week* (February 12, 1997), 38–39, and J. Johnson and S. Farkas, *Getting By: What American Teenagers Really Think about Their Schools* (New York: Public Agenda, 1997).

Students also offered reasonable advice for how they might attain such mastery. Two-thirds of the respondents said that students would learn more if they tried harder. About eight in 10 respondents said that students would learn more if schools made sure everyone was on time and completed all the homework assignments. More than seven in 10 said that schools should require after-school classes for anyone earning Ds or Fs. Students are not recommending that educational standards be lowered or that standardized testing programs be eliminated from public education. They seem to understand the importance of their own and others' learning.

Educators' Resistance to Standards and Testing

American educators are among the most severe critics of standards and testing programs. Despite poor test results, they maintain that public schools have high standards and are delivering acceptable academic results. For example, in response to the statement, "The school has high academic standards," seven in 10 principals and six in 10 teachers agreed, but only four in 10 students were convinced that high standards were being upheld in their school.

When considering the statement "The classes are challenging," seven in 10 principals and five in 10 teachers agreed, but only two in 10 students held such positive beliefs about their educational experiences. Educators' views obviously differ greatly from those of the public and students

Similarly, education professors who prepare aspiring and in-service teachers and administrators report opinions that differ sharply from those of the public and students. In national surveys, 78 percent of the faculty in colleges of education said they would like to see less reliance on multiple-choice examinations.[12] Only 24 percent believed it is "absolutely essential"

---

12. Steve Farkas and Jean Johnson, *Different Drummers: How Teachers of Teachers View Public Education* (New York: Public Agenda, 1997). www.publicagenda.org/reports/different-drummers; Steve Farkas and Ann Duffet, *Cracks in the Ivory Tower: The Views of Education Professors Circa 2010* (Washington, DC: Thomas B. Fordham Institute and FDR Group, 2010). For a summary of several content analyses of school of education reading lists carried by several scholars, see also Herbert J. Walberg, *Advancing Student Achievement* (Stanford, CA: Hoover Institution Press, 2010), 6–10.

to produce "teachers who understand how to work with the state's standards, tests, and accountability systems."

Their course outlines, reading assignments, and grading rubrics show indifference and even hostility toward using specific course objectives and measuring student outcomes. Despite the vast literature (discussed subsequently) on the benefits of testing on learning, educators and especially the educators of educators generally do not support testing and standards. Their attitude aligns with some of the commonly held fallacies about standardized testing.

Learning Benefits of Tests

The benefits of testing far outweigh any disadvantages. Largely ignored by test critics and some educators are hundreds of well-designed studies, complete with comparison groups, showing the benefits of tests. This voluminous research has been conveniently compiled in reviews of the research literature and statistical analysis of findings across multiple studies ("meta-analysis").[13] The conclusions are as follows:

- Setting unambiguous goals and measuring progress substantially increase student motivation and performance in learning, sports, and work settings.
- In K–12 and college classes, testing as often as weekly or daily promotes frequent preparation, which leads to increased learning. (Teaching students to frequently assess their own progress is an ultimate goal.)
- Giving students detailed test results helps them spot their weaknesses, increases their learning, and reduces the potential for overconfidence.
- Learning is reinforced and enhanced by offering students details on what they have done well.

---

13. The summary here derives from an extensive chapter by Richard Phelps with many citations, "The Rich, Robust Research Literature on Testing's Achievement Benefits," in Richard P. Phelps, ed., *Defending Standardized Testing* (Mahwah, NJ: Lawrence Erlbaum Associates, 2005), 55–90.

- Using tests to verify that students have mastered or nearly mastered specific content before introducing new material yields better results than teaching that ignores students' mastery levels.
- When studies focus on language learning, frequent testing has intensified and increased the speed with which students learn new languages.

Curriculum-Based External Tests

In addition to the comparison-group studies largely by psychologists, large-scale, statistically controlled studies of states and nations show that, on average, students who are required to pass standards- or curriculum-based examinations perform better than students who do not. Such tests cover uniform subject matter in humanities, sciences, and other fields. The tests are graded by educators other than the students' own teachers, and students have little incentive to challenge their teachers about course content and standards.

Rather, students and teachers work together toward their joint goal of meeting standards, which often have high stakes such as graduation and university admission. Because the exams and courses are uniform, teachers can concentrate on how to teach—not on what to teach. Knowing the subject matter in previous grades, teachers can build upon what students have previously been taught. Given all these findings, the benefits of testing appear to be as well established empirically as any principle in the social sciences.

As indicated earlier, John Bishop has closely studied and found positive effects of externally graded tests geared toward prescribed subject matters, such as the Advanced Placement, New York State Regents, and Canadian provincial examinations. According to Bishop, students required to take these exams perform nearly a full year ahead of other comparable students.[14]

---

14. John H. Bishop, "The Impact of Curriculum-based External Examinations on School Priorities and Student Learning," *International Journal of Educational Research*, 1996, vol. 23, no. 8, 653–752.

Massively extending Bishop's findings, Ludger Woessmann[15] of the Institute of World Economics carried out perhaps the largest and most sophisticated causal analysis of national achievement ever done. Using data from 39 countries that participated in the Third International Mathematics and Science Study, he found that students in rich and poor nations learned the most when their countries employed external, curriculum-based examinations.

Fallacies about Standardized Tests

Gregory Cizek points out several frequent, but fallacious, criticisms of standardized tests.[16] Despite the lack of foundation, these ideas are repeated so often that they deserve consideration and rebuttal.

Fallacy no. 1: Testing consumes valuable time that would otherwise be used for instruction.

Testing is inherently a part of instruction, not separate from it. Lectures, discussion activities, and assigned readings are useful. However, teachers must determine if the students have actually learned course material and proceed accordingly to re-teach or move on. Frequent, even daily testing encourages students to be prepared for each class rather than "cramming" easily forgotten information after infrequent tests. When tests match curricular standards, they reinforce students' learning by requiring them to think through and practice material they have completely or partially learned.

Two comparative studies conducted by John Bishop of Cornell University provide evidence of the instructional value of standardized tests.

---

15. Ludger Woessman, "Schooling Resources, Educational Institutions, and Student Performance: the International Evidence," *Oxford Bulletin of Economics and Statistics*, 2003, 2, 117–170; see also Eric A. Hanushek and Ludger Woessmann, "The Economics of International Differences in Educational Achievement" (conference paper delivered at CESIFO, Munich, Germany, September 2009).

16. Gregory J. Cizek, "High-Stakes Testing: Contexts, Characteristics, Critiques, and Consequences," in Richard P. Phelps, ed., *Defending Standardized Testing* (Mahwah, NJ: Lawrence Erlbaum Associates, 2005), 23–54. As an example of critics, Cizek cites Louis Smith and Clyde Rottenberg's article "Unintended Consequences of External Testing in Elementary Schools," *Educational Measurement: Issues And Practices*, 1991, *10* (4), 7–11.

In one study, he found that countries requiring students to take nationally standardized tests showed higher test scores on international tests than those in countries not requiring such tests.[17]

In a second study, Bishop found that U.S. students who anticipated having to pass an examination for high school graduation learned more science and math, were more likely to complete homework and talk with their parents about schoolwork, and watched less television than their peers who were not required to pass such exams.[18] These constructive activities encourage students to concentrate on meeting standards and monitoring their own time and progress—skills important for not only increased achievement but also increased success in life.

Fallacy no. 2: Testing programs consume sizable financial resources that would otherwise be used for instruction.

Standardized tests are not only effective but also are cost-efficient and represent only a minuscule percentage of K–12 expenditures. Caroline Hoxby found that in 2000, $234 million went to commercial firms for services including standardized testing, standards setting, and accountability reporting. This amount was less than 0.1 percent of total spending on K–12 education, and amounted to an average of only $5.81 per student. Across the 25 states with available information, the total cost per student was between $1.79 and $34.02.[19]

It is true, however, that states and school districts have paid steadily and substantially more over the past decade to devise their own tests. But lacking test and testing expertise, they have poor records of test effectiveness and cost-efficiency.[20] Backed by long records of experience and success

17. John H. Bishop, "The Effect of Curriculum-based External Exam Systems on Student Achievement," *Journal of Economic Education*, 1998, *29*, 171–182.

18. John H. Bishop, "Curriculum-based External Exam Systems: Do Students Learn More? How?" *Psychology, Public Policy, and Law*, 2000, *6*, 199–215.

19. Caroline M. Hoxby, "The Cost of Accountability" in Williamson M. Evers and Herbert J. Walberg, eds., *School Accountability* (Stanford, CA: Hoover Institution Press, 2002), 47–74.

20. Richard P. Phelps, "Estimating the Cost of Standardized Student Testing in the United States," *Journal of Education Finance*, 2000, *25*, 343–380.

in the marketplace, commercial tests are often more objective and reliable than the tests that states and smaller localities have commissioned.

In addition, well-made commercial tests can yield excellent diagnostic results in improving achievement by identifying student strengths and weaknesses. Commercial tests, moreover, are increasingly administered by computer and over the Internet, and their costs can be expected to continue declining.

Fallacy no. 3: Content not covered by tests is neglected.

It is true that holding educators accountable for only mathematics and language arts may lead them to neglect history and science. But this point is an argument for comprehensive and systematic testing across the entire curriculum.[21] Responsible test-makers, moreover, do not purport to cover all the material the students are expected to learn. Tests sample only a small fraction, perhaps as little as 5 or 10 percent, of all the content and skills.

Just as a national survey may interview a few tenths of a percent of the population, a 50-minute multiple-choice test of perhaps 50 items provides a good estimate of a student's overall achievement. Like a national survey designed to sample various parts of the country, moreover, a standardized test can sample the multiple topics students are expected to learn. Thus, such tests can sample far more content than a few essay questions.

Fallacy no. 4: Tests overemphasize factual knowledge and low-level skills.

Well-designed standardized tests can measure knowledge, understanding, application of ideas, and other high-level skills.[22] Designers can use single items with a clear, correct answer to assess lower level skills. They also can combine items and ask respondents to select the best answer when assessing complex knowledge.[23] Tests assessing complex achievement require respondents to select the best idea from a group of different and com-

---

21. More details are evident in Gregory J. Cizek, *Setting Performance Standards: Concepts, Methods, and Perspectives* (Mahwah, NJ: Lawrence Erlbaum Associates, 2001).

22. Norman Frederiksen, "The Real Test Bias: Influences of Testing on Teaching and Learning," *American Psychologist*, 1984, *39*, 193–202.

23. Norman E. Gronlund and C. Keith Waugh, *Assessment of Student Achievement*, 9th edition (Boston, MA: Allyn and Bacon, 2008).

pelling positions and require respondents to identify the best reason for action, the best interpretation of a set of ideas, or the best application of important principles. (Rather than the word "correct," "best" is advisable because more than one answer may be correct to some degree.)

Whereas tests emphasizing single, correct answers are common for students in early grades or who are new to an area of study, a wider range of items requiring interpretation are found on more advanced tests. K–12 students who practice demonstrating their knowledge and skills on standardized tests throughout their school career become better prepared to meet future educational, occupational, and professional goals. They are ready for the standardized tests assessing complex achievement that are used for admission to selective colleges and graduate and professional schools. In addition, K–12 students are prepared for tests required for occupational licensing for trades as well as for intellectually demanding professions such as law and medicine. The American Board of Internal Medicine, for example, uses multiple-choice, standardized tests to assess physicians' judgment before they can be certified in this advanced medical specialty.[24]

Fallacy no. 5: Testing places excessive pressure on students.

The world outside school is demanding. Indeed, the knowledge economy increasingly demands more knowledge and higher skills of workers, which require larger amounts of intense study of difficult subjects. Yet American students spend only about half the total study time of Asian students in regular schools, in tutoring schools, and in homework, making it unlikely that American students can academically compete with their global peers.[25] Thus, some pressure is advisable for the future welfare of the students and the nation.

When students can see their progress toward attaining standards, undue pressure can be mitigated and incremental progress can be motivating. As in games and sports, practice and frequent performance measures can enhance performance.[26] Just as difficulty levels established in recreational activities are common, testing programs allow educators to accommodate their curriculum to better meet the needs of students with

---

24. According to Timothy Sares, the board's director of testing.

25. Susan Paik, Debbie Wang, and Herbert J. Walberg, "Timely Improvements in Learning," *Educational Horizons,* 2002, *80,* 69–71.

26. Carol Dweck, *Mindset: The New Psychology of Success* (New York, NY: Random House, 2006).

different achievement levels.[27] Teachers can use test results to identify and respond directly to the specific needs of individual students by giving special help to those who fall behind and accelerating or enriching learning for advanced students.

Fallacy no. 6: Testing fosters malaise among all teachers.

Good schools focus on student learning, not on the satisfaction of the professional staff. If data shows that testing benefits students, it should be pursued even if there isn't unanimous teacher support. But professionals should take pride in seeing good results from their work, and because testing reveals good work and aids rather than detracts from instruction, teachers should embrace it.

Much of teacher dissatisfaction with testing is due to a lack of familiarity with why testing is necessary and how good tests are designed and administered. Often, a particular teacher's opposition is based on a past experience in which the test was poorly designed, not aligned with the curriculum, or in some other way incorrectly designed. Professional development programs that include guidance on how to align classroom tests with achievement standards can address these problems.[28] In one study, teachers were able to see the shortcomings of tests they designed and, thus, see how to devise better tests.[29]

Good student performance on tests should be a source of satisfaction among successful teachers, and the appropriate tests reveal strengths and weaknesses in the curriculum and instruction. Poor achievement progress shows that substantial improvements are needed in teaching and learning.

27.   Melissa Roderick and Mimi Engel, "The Grasshopper and the Ant: Motivational Responses of Low-Achieving Students to High-Stakes Testing," *Education Evaluation and Policy Analysis*, 2001, *23*, 197–227.

28.   Thomas R. Guskey, *Evaluating Professional Development* (Thousand Oaks, CA: Corwin, 2000).

29.   A.R. Gullickson and M.C. Ellwein, "Post-hoc Analysis of Teacher-made Tests: The Goodness of Fit Between Prescription and Practice," *Educational Measurement Issues and Practice*, 1985, *4*, 15–18.

3

WELL-MADE TESTS

Tests are a crucial element of a metaphorical three-legged stool that also includes standards and learning.[1] When one leg is missing or poorly executed, educational programs are likely to be faulty and learning is likely to proceed slowly or fail. Tests themselves can fail for two reasons—design and use. This chapter concerns the design of tests and the means of evaluating them and begins with a discussion of the key terms. Subsequent chapters describe the ideal and faulty uses of tests in policy and in school practices.

Validity

To ensure that tests can be used appropriately, especially in cases of major decisions such as high school graduation, college admission, and closing poorly performing schools, several validity criteria described in this chapter should be considered long before facing such decisions. Along with other considerations, the criteria can guide the selection or development of tests. Though the subject of achievement test validity is technical, policy-makers and parents can understand the criteria for the effective design and use of tests. Regrettably, practicing educators often lack technical knowledge of

---

1. For a comparative analysis of state systems, see Richard W. Cross, Theodor Rebarber, Justin Torres, and Chester E. Finn Jr., *Grading the Systems: The Guide to State Standards, Tests, and Accountability Policies* (Washington, DC: Thomas B. Fordham Foundation, January 2004).

validity covered in this chapter, and they may benefit from the summary offered here. The citations should be useful for a deeper technical understanding of the criteria, which are discussed in this chapter.

The term validity, as generally used here, means the test measures what it purports to measure; it is suited for or is aligned with the standards of the curriculum, course, or program in question. In a sense, standards should determine the nature and content of tests, and the two should be simultaneously considered. Since good tests require good standards, Chapter 8 is devoted to standards and their relation to tests.

Much of this book concentrates on tests used for major school decisions such as determining whether a student proceeds to the next grade or graduates from high school. Since the adoption of the No Child Left Behind legislation, test results can also influence whether or not a state puts a school on notice for failure to make "adequate yearly progress," and, in principle, repeated failure can lead to school closures or replacing the staff. Ordinary classroom tests, on the other hand, usually entail much less preparation and are often used only once. A student who does poorly on one day's test might make up for it another day.

Reliability

Reliability is analogous to the consistency of a ruler measuring length. A reliable ruler doesn't stretch; it yields the same or nearly the same measurement each time it is applied to the same object. In one sense, standardized tests can be considered reliable when the same test given twice or alternate forms of the same test yield nearly the same ranking of students. Students who score high on one occasion should score high on the same test given on a second occasion soon after. A test, of course, may be highly reliable but lack validity since it measures mastery other than what is specified in the standards just as a reliable ruler can invalidly measure the wrong dimension of a box.

Multiple-choice tests on average are considerably more reliable than essays and performance assessments. In ranking student essays and speeches, for example, judges' assessments often differ substantially.[2] One judge may

---

2. The lack of agreement among essay graders has long been recognized. See, for example, Verner Martin Sims, "Reducing the Variability of Essay Examination Marks Through Eliminating Variations of Standards of Grading," *Journal of Educational Research*, May 1933, vol. 26, no. 9, 637–648.

assign an A, and another may assign a D. When the grades are used for high-stakes decisions, several judges are typically used and their grades are averaged. Using several judges, however, is costly and time-consuming.

Standardization

A standardized test presents identical or similar tasks to students under the same conditions, particularly the time allowed for completion. Just as comparing running times for sporting events would be misleading if the track lengths differed, test scores obtained under unstandardized conditions cannot be reasonably compared. Nor can they be used for defensible decisions about group members.

Standardization is a complex matter even in seemingly simple cases and can entail unanticipated problems that undermine validity. Typing provides a good example. A standard calling for typing 50 words a minute, for example, might require an identical keyboard for all examinees; but some typists may have practiced on similar keyboards, giving them an advantage over others. Similarly, the text to be typed should be identical for all, but some may find the text and practice typing it beforehand. Random texts may yield unstandardized difficulty levels; technical texts, for example, may be more difficult to type than common prose.

Such problems often arise in measuring knowledge and skills. High-quality tests minimize these problems by using careful design, independent review of items by experts and experienced teachers, pilot trials of the items with students, and informed revisions. Since standardized commercial tests in such subjects as English language skills, mathematics, and science undergo such steps, they are usually highly correlated. That is, a student who scores well on a mathematics tests of one test publisher is likely to do well on another publisher's test of the same subject. Such correlations are attributable to the tendency of test publishers to test what is commonly taught in schools; the tests are valid in that they generally reflect largely agreed-upon subject matter and skills.

Classroom Testing and Learning Time

Testing requires a fraction of the total time allocated for instruction. Some critics argue that testing time reduces learning time, but this contention is misleading for several reasons. Tests generally require students to recall or apply what they have learned often in ways that they had not previously thought about. This can reinforce, deepen, and extend learning.

Tests, moreover, show students and teachers what has been learned well and poorly, information that should guide relearning and new goal setting. In fact, studies have consistently shown, as discussed in Chapter 2, that frequent tests with results provided promptly produce better learning. Regular testing can also encourage students to stay prepared for class rather than cramming for less frequent tests, which results in quicker forgetting. Testing and instruction are out of balance at two extremes: if teachers literally teach students how to answer specific questions on the test ("teaching the test") or if instructional activities have no connection with the achievement measured by the test, both of which should be determined by standards.

Creating Incentives for Performing Well

Incentives powerfully influence behavior, but they should not be uncritically assumed.[3] It can be generally assumed that candidates for admission to selective colleges and for occupational and professional licensing are strongly motivated to succeed; they face serious consequences for failure. However, students participating in state, national, and international testing programs may know that their scores will not affect their grades, and neither their teachers nor their parents will see their results. As a consequence, they may not put forth their best effort, thereby undermining the validity of the results.

Thus, students may be indifferent to achievement tests such as the National Assessment of Educational Progress and state testing programs that count for nothing on their grades, college admission, and careers. The solution, as discussed in several places in this book, is to provide constructive incentives that induce students to do their best and to ensure greater validity of test results. Among these ways is allowing high-scoring students to graduate early from high school and awarding them merit scholarships to college.

---

3. Steven D. Levitt and Stephen J. Dubner, *Freakonomics: A Rogue Economist Explores the Hidden Side of Everything* (NY: Harper Perennial, 2009) [Originally published in 2005].

Maximizing Test Security

To help ensure that a test is externally valid, the test must be kept secure before and after administration. If some students know test questions in advance, this knowledge can invalidate comparisons among test takers. For this reason, high-stakes tests are often kept under lock and key, and other security precautions are taken to ensure that students cannot learn the content of a test beforehand and share that knowledge with others.

Even with seemingly sure security, the content of any test repeated year after year becomes known by some students, which allows them to memorize the answers without really mastering the intended knowledge and skills, thereby invalidating the results. One solution is to create a new test for each occasion, but this requires complicated and controversial calibration procedures if the test results are to be compared across years. Another solution is to build large repositories of items ("item banks") that align well with standards but are too voluminous for a given student to master all the answers without actually knowing the material.

Test Preparation

Before drafting items, test developers draw up a blueprint that follows the standards. The number of items for each section of the test reflects the importance of the subject and skills in the standards. A reading test for the later grades is likely to contain a preponderance of comprehension items in contrast to word recognition, consonant blending, and other skills emphasized in the early grades. The sample of items is analogous to small survey samples of large populations in that the sample of items serves to estimate what students know about the subject as a whole as called for by the standards. In one sense, the test design may be said to be valid to the extent that the blueprint follows the standards and their component parts.

Test validity can be subjectively assessed by determining the degree to which it serves the purpose for which it was designed. A test designed to measure mathematics skills, for example, is unlikely to be a valid indicator of students' knowledge of history. To conclude the math test is valid, test developers may hire subject matter experts who assess the degree that each item aligns with the standards. The judges of mathematics items may include not only mathematics teachers and professors but also engineers and scientists who use mathematics in their work.

Before and during this work, there may be reasons for debate and clarification about the purpose and the nature of the standards for given students. For example, "word problem" items on a mathematics test may demand knowledge of words beyond some students' vocabulary even though they have mastered mathematics and its application in simply expressed language. Thus, if the test is to measure mathematics achievement alone, the items must be rewritten. On the other hand, perhaps the standards require rethinking and clarification.[4]

As emphasized in Chapters 5, 6, and 7, motivation, cheating, and clever test takers can undermine test validity. If, for example, students put forth varying amounts of effort, their test scores will be partly a function of their varying degrees of motivation. Varying amounts of cheating will be partial determinants of test scores, thereby reducing validity. Badly designed tests can similarly undermine validity. Such tests, for example, often have the second of several answers as preponderantly the correct alternative. Clever students may notice this tendency and, when uncertain, choose the second answer as the more probable. Thus, the test measures to some extent test-taking ability rather than the intended knowledge and skills called for in the standards.

---

4. Since this book concentrates on school achievement tests, it omits descriptions of concurrent and predictive validity, often at issue in admission, occupational, and licensing tests. These forms of validity are indicated by the quantitative degree of correlation of the test scores with current performance or, in the case of selection tests, with later success. Used for selection of university students, for example, the Scholastic Aptitude Test (SAT) predicts 10 to 20 percent of the variation in their grade-point averages. Similarly, occupational selection tests predict a small amount of the variance in on-the-job success but are more valid than other indicators such as ratings based on interviews. It cannot be claimed that admission tests are good predictors of college grades nor that licensing tests predict occupational success well since success depends on many hard-to-measure factors, such as perseverance and the ability to get along well with others. An old college joke has it that A students become professors and that B students wind up working for C students.

4

TYPES AND USES OF ACHIEVEMENT TESTS

In a paper titled "The Real Test Bias," Norman Frederikson called attention to the possible mismatch of test characteristics to the user's goals particularly with respect to standards.[1] A match may not be easily accomplished over the long term since national and state standards change, and even the vocabulary of textbooks, other instructional media, and the tests themselves may become obsolete and need to be changed. In addition, as considered in this chapter, different types of achievement tests serve distinctive purposes and users, and no single test can well serve all purposes and users. So, the uses and types of achievement tests deserve specification and description here.

Purposes of Tests

Three major purposes of tests are worth considering, though they overlap one another somewhat. Each type, however, may be most useful only for the purposes it is intended to address and, as explained in the previous chapter, it may be sufficiently valid and reliable only for its intended purpose.

Diagnostic tests

These tests are used to assess the needs of individuals or of programs, districts, and other features of an educational system. Diagnostic tests are

---

1. Norman Frederikson, "The Real Test Bias: Influences of Testing on Teaching and Learning." *American Psychologist,* 1984, *39*, 193–202.

used to identify the specific strengths and weakness of individual students, classrooms, or schools.

Formative tests

Similar to diagnostic tests, formative tests are given frequently, perhaps even daily, to assess individual student and class progress in attaining relatively short-term goals related to the standards.[2] Traditionally they are in the form of a quiz intended to help teachers and students assess their progress. Frequent quizzes not only provide such feedback, but, if graded, also encourage students to be prepared for each of their class sessions.

Skillful teachers may quiz their students orally to probe their knowledge, skills, and understanding. Adept teachers may weave such formative assessments so smoothly into the rest of the classroom activities that students hardly know their performance is being assessed. Students may be asked to display their work, explain the reasoning behind answers, or outline their thinking, possibly using the blackboard or other physical objects. Thus, formative tests and oral assessments are intended to provide information needed to guide classroom instruction well enough to ensure the attainment of course objectives.

Summative tests

Summative tests are usually given less often than the other two kinds, but they typically assess a broader range of knowledge and skills than formative tests. They often require students to integrate newly acquired learning with old learning. Challenging criteria for establishing reliability and validity are typically adopted for summative tests largely because these tests are commonly used to assign course grades and to report progress to parents and school authorities.

Summative tests generate controversy because they are often used for accountability and to compare teachers, schools, districts, states, and nations, some of which, by definition, must be below average. Summative

---

2. Catherine S. Taylor and Susan Bobbitt Nolen, *Classroom Assessment: Supporting Teaching and Learning in Real Classrooms* (Upper Saddle River, NJ: Pearson Education, 2008).

tests are increasingly used for high-stakes decisions such as allowing a student to proceed to the next grade level, graduate with honors, or even graduate at all. Schools may be put on a "watch list" or even closed because too few of their students are proficient or fail to make progress. Since mistakes may be tragic and controversy and litigation may ensue, summative tests should be unquestionably valid and reliable and procedurally defensible.

Types of Tests

As described in the preceding section, diagnostic and formative tests are largely within the province of educators. They can use the results to improve their programs and help students to exploit their strengths and make progress in their areas of weakness. On a daily or weekly basis, however, they may share detailed results with parents who can then encourage their children's progress and help them with problems they may be having.

As consumers, parents are as concerned with their children's overall progress as are citizens, school board members, and legislators in meeting their responsibility to hold educators accountable for results. For this reason, these groups are usually focused on summative tests that inform them of how individual children, teachers, schools, and districts rank. Since they tend to be inherently more objective, reliable, and valid, multiple-choice tests, as explained in this section, are usually preferred for educational consumers and for those that provide oversight.

Multiple-choice tests

Multiple-choice tests are commonly considered to be the gold standard for standardized testing, although they have been misleadingly called recognition tests because they are said to require students only to recognize which of several alternatives is the best answer. Students who score well on recognition and factual items also tend to score well on other parts of tests that involve "higher processes" such comprehension and the application of ideas.[3] Similarly, we expect that great composers and instrumentalists

---

3. Thomas M. Haladyna, Steven M. Downing, and Michael C. Rodriguez, "A Review of Multiple-Choice Item-Writing Guidelines in Classroom Assessment," *Applied Measurement in Education*, 2002, *15*, 309–334.

have learned to read musical scores before they exhibit their higher talents. Similarly, learning arithmetic usually precedes mastery of trigonometry and calculus.

Contrary to antitesting ideology discussed in Chapters 1 and 2, scholars and test developers have shown it is possible for well-designed multiple-choice items to measure more than isolated, memorized facts. Items can be constructed to address many aspects of critical thinking, such as the ability to create and evaluate novel solutions, synthesize seemingly discrepant information, and analyze and reorganize the elements of problems to arrive at solutions. Although the absence of factual knowledge is usually a quick and sure sign of missing expertise in any specialty, multiple-choice items can accurately and cost-effectively capture many aspects of high-level thinking objectively, reliably, and validly.

None of this is to say that multiple-choice tests are faultless. As pointed out in Chapter 2, sizable numbers of educators oppose them and the student and educator accountability they imply. Some of their criticisms, moreover, hold up against poorly designed multiple-choice tests that untrained educators themselves often offer. Amateurishly designed tests, for example, often contain a preponderance of items in which the correct answer is B, the second option. When drafting the test, untrained authors often give the first option the first incorrect answer that comes to mind, and then to avoid forgetting to include the correct answer makes it the second, followed by several incorrect answers. To counter such problems, expert test developers use random numbers to determine where the correct answer lies in the sequence of options.

As explained in the next chapter, professional test developers and some educators take several steps to avoid such problems. In the end, well-designed multiple-choice tests cannot be matched in objectivity, reliability, and validity—the major reasons they are widely used for admission to college, graduate and professional schools, and occupational and professional licensing programs in such fields as law and medicine.

Essay tests

Essay tests are said to probe students' recall of information because respondents must remember the correct answers or construct answers from points recalled from memory. Such tests may also assess students' ability to marshal arguments and write coherent prose. For these reasons, there seems no effective substitute for assigning, carefully critiquing, and grading essays and term papers—and requiring improved rewriting. Frequent writing in classrooms and in homework provides the practice required to improve writing skills.

Despite their instructional advantages, essay tests are difficult to construct well and costly to score objectively for summative purposes, even with newly available computer tools for evaluating text, such as the spelling and grammar checker in Microsoft Word. Because essay tests are usually composed of only a few questions, they typically sample a narrower range of a subject than multiple-choice tests, which may have several dozen items. Another potential problem of essay tests is that they fail to measure mastery of specific content but unintentionally tap general knowledge and writing skill. Thus, a clever wordsmith can mislead graders.

Students also devise ways to avoid the mastery essay tests are designed to assess. By memorizing major themes from study guides, they sometimes can do well without actually reading assigned works. Essay questions are sometimes required for high-stakes college admission tests, but these, too, are subject to invalidity since application essays can be purchased on the Internet and possibly adapted to answer a distinctive admission question. (Because of these problems, admission committees, for better or worse, sometimes give more weight to personal interviews and claimed experiences such as volunteering as a tutor, helping at a hospital, setting sports records, and other unusual accomplishments. These, too, are laden with error and subjectivity.)

A final problem with essay examinations is their general unreliability attributable to the subjectivity of judging good writing. In judging essays, for example, one grader may give an essay an A while another gives a D. This lack of agreement can be solved in part by using a detailed protocol for judging each essay question or by averaging the judges' grades. These solutions, however, are time-consuming and expensive.

For these reasons, essay tests are rarely weighed in assessments on which major decisions are based, such as occupational licensing and admission to college and graduate and professional schools. The notable exceptions are schools of journalism and other fields in which writing is the main craft. Even in these cases, a portfolio of writing samples rather than a single administered essay are preferred because they offer a larger sample of performance. Even so, assignment and grading of essays for instruction should be a major part of student experience since writing is essential for a good education, many occupations, and other aspects of adult life.

Portfolio assessments

Educators and others sometimes use portfolio assessments to encourage students to display samples of their work, notably in creative writing, photography, and other visual arts.[4] Portfolios are less desirable for assessing students' work in the usual academic subjects and skills because they lack objectivity, reliability, validity, and cost-efficiency. Decisions about what to include in a portfolio undermine attempts to draw objective comparisons among students and with respect to standards. Students and their parents and mentors may, for example, select their best work for the portfolio and discard weak examples. It may be difficult, too, to ensure that the samples are the student's actual work.

Similarly, scoring protocols can be constructed to evaluate an individual's portfolio, but they typically rely on highly subjective, time-consuming, and often disparate judgments. Portfolios require more storage and organization across a school year than would be the case for summative, standardized tests used to document students' achievement. Portfolios are costly to rank, and their evaluation may be unfair unless those who have no stake in the results judge them. In short, portfolios offer excellent ways to exhibit a student's idiosyncratic record of work in limited areas, but they prove far less useful in determining their school, state, and national achievement standings.

Performance assessments

Current and former students may need to demonstrate skills that cannot be accurately measured with multiple-choice and essay tests. Skills that require creativity, artistry, interpersonal communication, or leadership are

---

4. Bill Johnson, *Performance Assessment Handbook, Volume 1: Portfolios and Socratic Seminars* (Princeton, NJ: Eye on Education, 1996).

difficult to measure reliably and validly. Students may need to actually exhibit public speaking, diving, painting, acting, piano playing, or other observable skills to be assessed by judges.[5]

Such performance assessments, however, include errors. A single coach can give day-to-day or minute-by-minute formative assessments, but multiple judges are commonly used to rate the same high-stakes events such as championships, and the averages of the judges are usually taken. These performance assessments are costly since they require several expert raters to maintain reliability and validity. In contrast, when outcomes are assessed using multiple-choice items, thousands of tests can be machine-scored in minutes for a fraction of a cent each.

Item Delivery Systems

Although debates about the role of testing in education have waxed and waned for as long as tests have been available, technologies for administering tests and facilitating greater levels of standardization have moved forward decisively. Computers have become more widely available, and procedures for administering tests, recording scores, and comparing findings continue to become easier and more prevalent. Educational tests are currently administered three ways.

Paper-and-pencil tests

The design of standardized paper-and-pencil tests involves complex decisions about where to put items on a page and the order of placement for different sections. Such tests are commonly used in a wide range of settings, largely because they do not require special technology to administer and are usually easily managed by the examinees. Machine scoring is available for evaluating large numbers of tests, and this method of administration seems versatile enough for most students of different ages and abilities.

---

5. Performance in sports is different since winning points can be compiled and track events can be precisely timed. The immense interest in sports may reflect the excitement generated by such objective numbers, which are often immediately available, though measuring an individual's contribution in team sports is difficult.

When paper-and-pencil tests are used for large-scale testing programs, a number of problems can arise, including printing the tests incorrectly, distributing them without needed security, and delaying the mailing of the answer sheets and their results—all of which can entail errors, costs, and delays. The sheer bulk of paper can create logistical challenges that need to be thoughtfully solved beforehand. Scoring standardized essay examinations entails further complications. Subject matter graders may need to be recruited and trained. Typically if two graders differ by more than two points on a five-point scale, a third grader is required to resolve the difference.

Computer-administered adaptive tests

The origins of adaptive testing are traceable to Alfred Binet who, shortly after 1900, developed a standardized test to identify students who lacked the ability to profit from the regular school curriculum in France. Some students already understood most of what was being taught whereas others consistently lagged behind, and Binet wanted to understand why. Translated by Lewis Terman at Stanford University and published in 1916, the Stanford-Binet tests were widely used in the U.S. to estimate students' IQs (intelligence quotients or the ratio of mental age to chronological age, now rarely used).

Binet employed "adaptive" administration methods, as did subsequent individually administered intelligence tests. If a student failed to answer an item correctly, an easier item was given. More difficult items followed correct answers, and the test procedure continuously adapted to the individual student's ability. Because of the high cost of individually administered Stanford-Binet and subsequent adaptive tests, most tests (including nearly all achievement tests used in American K–12 schools) did not follow Binet's precedent. School district administrators selected a commercial paper-and-pencil test, and all students[6] in a given grade within the district took the test.

Today, however, adaptive tests, which save time and money, are increasingly being administered by computer and over the Internet. Items are

---

6. With the exception of students designated as having special needs, such as those with severely limited vision.

stored in large databases or "item banks,"[7] and a student's performance on each item is used to select subsequent items most suitable to the increasingly well-estimated ability level. As in Binet's precedent, passing a given item leads to the administration of more difficult items, and failure to pass an item leads to the administration of easier items. An adaptive test that selects as few as 15 items can be as reliable as a 60-item paper-and-pencil test, and a computer can report a student's score as soon as the test is completed. Analyses of each student's strengths and weaknesses and similar analyses for each grade and subject for whole classes and schools can follow in a day or two.

Adaptive tests are commonly used for admission to college and graduate and professional schools, and are slowly replacing paper-and-pencil tests. Examples are the Scholastic Aptitude Test, the Graduate Record Examinations, and, for schools, the widely used Northwest Evaluation Association tests. Because items are selected from large item banks and because the tests are time-efficient, it is possible to administer them as many as four times a year in contrast to the usual administration of only an annual examination.

Integrated classroom tests

Just as computers made it possible to adapt high-stakes tests to the abilities of the examinee, they make it more practical to fully integrate testing and learning. Integrated testing approaches emerged from the discovery that the longer the delay between taking a test and learning the results, the less likely the learner will benefit from the feedback. Without clear and immediate feedback, students may continue to perpetuate mistakes that can be difficult to eradicate later.

Given that immediate feedback promotes learning, integrated testing has become a major component of computerized tutoring programs. Computer programs offer increasingly sophisticated methods for presenting

---

7.   Item banks are large collections of items numbering in the hundreds or thousands from which tests can be assembled. In principle, it would be possible to make these banks publicly accessible since students could not memorize all the items, nor would educators and students know which ones would be used on any particular testing occasion. Since each student takes items most suitable for his or her ability and students sitting near one another take different sets of items, cheating is minimized. Educators, moreover, cannot easily cheat on such tests.

content in small chunks and immediately testing students' mastery. They measure fine-grain progress, item by item, and students are immediately informed of the correctness of their responses.

When students give a wrong answer, computer programs offer opportunities to review the material, present it in a different way, or return to prerequisite material. After sufficient student accomplishment, the program verifies mastery and assesses the degree to which skills can be applied to new situations. When tests are closely coordinated with learning progress and the standards, students see their progress and the value of immediate and accurate feedback.

Standards-Based vs. Norm-Referenced Tests

Standardized achievement tests tend to fall into one of two major categories with somewhat different functions. Standards-based tests assess whether or not a student meets expert-defined standards for a particular age or grade level. Schools, districts, and states often report the *percentages* of students of a particular grade (or age) that have met a standard such as "Proficient."[8] Meeting the widespread Proficient standard typically means the student is prepared or preparing adequately to move to the next grade level. In some school systems, failure to meet the Proficiency standards results in grade retention or summer school.

Norm-referenced tests are designed to compare students with others in the same grade or age. The scores can be expressed several ways, with the most common being the *percentile*, which is the percentage of the students a particular student exceeds in performance. A student at the 50th percentile, for example, exceeds 50 percent of the norm group, usually a well-defined random sample of students from the nation.

The most efficient norm-referenced tests contain items on which about half[9] the students succeed and which yield scores that discriminate across

---

8. The governing board of the National Assessment of Educational Progress (NAEP) pioneered standards-based assessment and employed four levels—Below Basic, Basic, Proficient, and Advanced—in the major school subjects. Before this, mastery learning employed criterion-based tests for a set of lessons that a student had to pass with typically 80 percent correct answers before proceeding to increasingly challenging lessons.

9. To be precise, for a multiple-choice test with four options for each item, the ideal average item difficulty level is 62.5 percent.

a range from the lowest to the highest levels of achievement. Standards-based tests, however, might mean that nearly none or nearly all the students meet a particular standard, depending on their mastery and the rigor of the standard. Ideally, all or nearly all students can meet a challenging standard.[10]

Standards-based tests have long been used to select candidates for occupations and professions such as medicine. A growing number of school tests are standards-based because of the federal No Child Left Behind legislation, which requires schools to report adequate yearly progress, or increase in percentage of students that meet a given proficiency standard in the several grades and subjects tested. Since proficiency depends on students' achievement as well as state standards, a state may be able to report high percentages of proficient students merely because it has low standards, lower, for example, than those of other states and Asian and European countries. Considerable evidence suggests that the states generally set their standards too low, that is, considerably below the proficiency standards of the National Assessment of Educational Progress, which are more comparable to the standards of countries with advanced economies.[11]

E.D. Hirsch Jr. was one of the first scholars to point out the need for setting standards for each grade level so that a teacher at one level could depend on what students had been taught at previous levels.[12] To ensure grade-level mastery, standards-based tests are in principle well aligned with state standards. Indeed, standards also determine the goals of lessons, curricula, and instruction.

---

10. On pass-fail tests, meeting the standard means attaining the minimum score required for passing. Other tests may have multiple cut-point scores to specify more than one degree of proficiency, such as Below Basic, Basic, Proficient, and Advanced according to the NAEP.

11. Paul E. Peterson and Carlos Xabel Lastra-Anadon, "State Standards Rise in Reading, Fall in Math," *Education Next*, fall 2010, 12–14; National Center for Education Statistics, *Mapping 2005 State Proficiency Standards onto the NAEP Scales*, NCES 2007-482, (Washington, DC: U.S. Department of Education, National Center for Education Statistics, 2007). Test analyses, such as this, are often published years after the tests are given because of slow statistical processing times.

12. See, for example, E.D. Hirsch Jr., *The Schools We Need and Why We Don't Have Them* (New York: Doubleday, 1996).

5

PREPARING STANDARDIZED ACHIEVEMENT TESTS

Given the types of achievement tests and the means of evaluating them described in Chapters 3 and 4, this chapter describes steps in designing and constructing high-quality tests. Also covered are the means of analyzing preliminary versions of tests, developing norms, setting cut scores[1] for standards-based tests, and reporting test results for various groups interested in them. This chapter concentrates on ideals of test preparation, which are seldom followed by teachers (and college professors), who are usually untrained in testing and may justifiably be less rigorous in the preparation of tests for one-time use with fewer than 100 students.

Planning Tests

Regardless of whether a standardized test is intended for norm-referenced or standards-based purposes, the planning stages are similar. Both require an initial "blueprint" just as in architecture. For standards-based tests, developers, working from a close review of the state standards, set forth a blueprint or matrix consisting of subject matter topics cross-classified with general mental processes such as knowledge acquisition, comprehension, application, and evaluation of ideas. For example, a cell in the matrix might include the application of physical ideas in comprehending

---

1. Cut scores are the minimum scores needed to attain specified degrees of proficiency such as Basic, Proficient, and Advanced. For pass-fail tests, however, meeting the standard means attaining the single minimum score required for passing.

a thunderstorm, identifying the causes of the civil war, and knowing and evaluating the features of a sonnet. Like most textbooks, norm-referenced blueprints are heavily based on what subject matter experts and teachers think should be generally taught in most grades in the nation.

In either case, the blueprint specifies the allocation or percentage of items to be drafted for each cell depending on their importance.[2] Once initially specified in these ways, the blueprints undergo cycles of scrutiny and revision, and eventual approval.

Drafting, Revising, and Selecting Items

Given the approved blueprint, test developers employ expert teams of item writers to draft databases or item banks aligned with the cells in the blueprint. They draft more items than will actually be used on the test for two reasons. Some items will not survive rigorous screening based on students' actual responses, and item banks may require as many as ten times the items so that they can be circulated in and out of subsequent test editions, particularly computer- and Internet-administered versions.

The items for well-crafted tests are placed in particular sequences to prevent clever test takers from inferring correct answers without having mastered the subject of study. A repeated question, for example, with the same correct answer but different incorrect answers enables some examinees to answer based on logic alone. Inexperienced test developers, including teachers and college professors, may leave other clues such as a tendency to make the second of four or five alternative answers the correct one so that rules such as "when in doubt, choose the second" may aid the ill-prepared student.

Rules can be set to eliminate such things in tests, but craft knowledge, experience, and intuition also remain useful. In any case, multiple critics review and rereview the draft items; some may be satisfactorily revised, others eliminated. By the time a set of items is provisionally finished, developers

---

2. As emphasized in Chapter 8, defective standards and blueprints usually lead to faulty tests.

have explored a multitude of potential sources of bias and invalidity. Even so, a few defective items may slip through the most careful screening.

Item Examples

Most standardized tests include multiple-choice items in which students are given a "stem" that raises a question and are asked to select from a variety of alternative answers. In well-designed tests, less desirable answers, called "distracters," are often written to help diagnose why students answer incorrectly, and the ideal or correct answer reflects the relatively best response to the stem. When multiple-choice items are used to determine the accuracy with which respondents can recognize information, comprehend the meaning of the material on the test, or apply knowledge to concrete situations, each item is independent of all others and requires students to select the correct answer from a range of choices.

Consider, for example, the following draft items in which individuals are asked to report their knowledge of a testing fact, understanding of a concept, and application of information to a particular situation.

Goal: Identify key testing terms.

The two most essential features of a standardized test are:

    A. Novelty and rigor.

  *B. Reliability and validity.

    C. Comprehensiveness and depth.

    D. Difficulty and complexity.

Goal: Illustrate a benefit of testing.

What is the key reason why students directly benefit from taking tests?

    A. Teachers can monitor students' behavior.

    B. Students are exposed to important skills.

    C. School districts can assess teaching effectiveness.

  *D. Students receive feedback on their learning.

Goal: Identify an ideal procedure for assessing knowledge.

Which of the following techniques offers the most efficient way of evaluating academic achievement for an entire course?

    A. Ask students to complete a portfolio of projects.

    B. Ask students to write an essay on a topic of their choice.

   *C. Ask students to complete standardized tests for each subject.

    D. Ask students to respond to short-answer questions.

A careful reader may debate the validity of these draft items and suggest improvements, though it is far easier to criticize items than to draft acceptable ones that make it through screening committees.

Multiple-choice items can also be used to determine how well individuals can interpret and respond to complex problems. When this is the test purpose, items are often clustered around a broader problem and respondents are asked to select the best answer from a range of reasonable alternatives. Consider the following interpretive exercise.

Goal: To assess what constitutes relevant evidence, knowledge of different types of tests, and the recognition of implicit assumptions.

Directions: Read the following passage about the state of education in the United States, and identify the best response to the stems below.

"Student achievement has been low and stagnant for a number of years. Rather than look for innovative ways to increase learning, educators often blame tests for conveying misleading information, for example, that standardized tests underestimate students' important learning. Perhaps if educators understood how tests are designed, they could better see the dangers of dismissing stagnant test scores."

Which of the following forms of evidence would best strengthen the author's message?

    A. Evidence showing that innovative teaching is taking place.

    B. A list of interesting educational policies.

    *C. Evidence that teachers do not understand tests and testing.

    D. Evidence that student test scores have not declined.

What kinds of tests are referred to in the above paragraph?

    *A. Standardized tests.

    B. Criterion-referenced, teacher-designed tests.

    C. Standardized, supply-item tests.

    D. Diagnostic, international tests.

Which of the following assumptions is also found in the above passage?

    A. Teachers have control over what students learn.

    *B. Teachers see tests as unrelated to learning.

    C. The role of school in society is well understood.

    D. Teachers find change invigorating.

The four- and five-choice multiple-choice items are the most frequently used item format on standardized tests, largely because of their versatility. Nevertheless, some learning outcomes are sufficiently narrow in scope that two-choice true-false items offer a useful format in tests. It may also be desirable for respondents to accurately associate one idea with another, such as states and their capitals, in which case matching items are more appropriate. Like other items, these formats can be easily machine-scored. Norman Gronlund and Keith Waugh compiled a wide range of guidelines for writing all types of test items.[3] They cite a wealth of literature comparing and contrasting the skills associated with answering different types of items that makes it possible to identify the evidenced-based strengths and limitations of different item formats.

Field Testing and Item Analysis

Carefully screened items undergo field evaluations to determine how well they work in practice with students. A preliminary version of the test may be given to several hundred students, and the student responses to the items are analyzed. The item difficulty, defined as the percentage of students who answer correctly,[4] can be a decisive indicator of item quality. If none or 100 percent of the students answered correctly on a standards-based test, it suggests the standard or its blueprint interpretation may be too high or too low, which expert panels may judge. Alternatively, the material may have been poorly taught. For norm-referenced tests, such items are generally useless since they contribute nothing to the discriminating sensitivity of the test.

A second indicator of possible item quality is discrimination, or the correlation of the item with the total score on the preliminary test. An item that high scorers tend to get wrong more often than low scorers is suspect. Perhaps there is a fallacious nuance in the item that only the best-prepared students see. Such items go to an expert panel for review, adjudication, and possible revision or deletion.

The incorrect item alternatives (called "distracters") are analyzed. If more than, say, 40 percent of examinees choose a single incorrect alternative, there may be a problem in the teaching material or in teaching since so many students are misled by the same presumably mistaken idea. It is also possible that the item itself is faulty. If none or few students choose a particular incorrect alternative, the alternative is not contributing to the discriminating sensitivity of the item and deserves review.

---

3. Norman E. Gronlund and C. Keith Waugh, *Assessment of Student Achievement*, 9th edition (Boston, MA: Allyn and Bacon, 2008).

4. Difficulty is a traditional but misleading descriptor since the higher the difficulty, that is, correct percentage, the easier the item.

Establishing Norms

Adequate sociological and political surveys require large random samples of, say, one or two thousand participants, to make reasonable inferences about a far larger and usually national population. Similar large samples are necessary for standardized tests for comparing students partly because the items are usually designed and selected for grade levels such as fourth through sixth, and each set of grade levels may require a separate sample. Besides other considerations, items comprising the tests are around 50 percent in difficulty level to afford maximum coverage of grades and to discriminate between high- and low-achieving students.

The sum of correct answers is the student's "raw score," determined by both the student's mastery and the number and difficulty of the items. The raw scores are usually converted to "transformed scores" for reporting to various audiences, including teachers, parents, and the students themselves. A common transformed score is the familiar percentile, which indicates the estimated place of the student in the sample and, by inference, the national population.

Setting Cut Scores for Standards

Where norm-referenced scores compare an examinee's mastery to that of other examinees who took the test, standards-based tests categorize an examinee at a given level of proficiency or standard such as the now common categories Basic, Proficient, and Advanced in the National Assessment of Educational Progress. (Many occupational tests have only one proficiency level or standard—pass). To set proficiency levels, subject matter experts and others estimate the probability that an examinee will correctly answer each item on the test at a given proficiency level. In one approach, the judges' ratings for each item are averaged and summed to identify the minimum score to attain a given proficiency level.[5] Though

---

5. For methods and complications of standards setting, see William H. Angoff, "Scales, Norms, and Equivalent Scores" in Robert L. Thorndike, ed., *Educational Measurement,* 2nd edition (Washington, DC: American Council on Education, 1971), 508–600, and Gregory J. Cizek, ed., *Setting Performance Standards: Concepts, Methods, and Perspectives* (Mahwah, NJ: Lawrence Erlbaum Associates, 2001).

cut-score setting for school tests can be objectively described, the process is subject to strong and often successful political pressure to maintain low levels to make proficiency appear better than it really is.

Reporting Results

Teachers can benefit from detailed results of tests, such as the percentage of students who pass each item, so that they can plan program revisions accordingly. Immediate or near immediate results are most useful so that teachers can make quick changes. This is a major advantage of computer administration and scoring of tests over traditional paper-and-pencil tests, which involve delays and costs associated with the mailing of score reports.

Legislators and citizens may be best served with overall scores or subscores in areas such as word recognition, vocabulary, and reading comprehension reported less frequently, perhaps only annually. They are likely to want comparisons of schools and districts, demographic groups, and recent and past results to measure progress. Parents will want to know where their children rank. Educators should desire all these plus detailed results on how their students perform on each item.

Unfortunately, test technicians often design reporting systems for print and Internet reports, which are ill suited to the needs and understanding of each group with their different interests. A common fault is an overwhelming amount of needlessly difficult-to-understand technical information. Multiple reports suited for the several intended audiences and improved with user surveys are needed.

Technology vs. Politics

The steps described comprise a well-developed technology that in principle leads to objective, reliable, and valid measurement of educational objectives. The setting of standards and cut scores, however, can be highly political. If left completely or largely to interested parties, namely defensive educators who wish to avoid accountability for their accomplishments, the standards and cut scores are likely to be lax. As a matter of human nature, few of us want to be evaluated by high, objective standards. The marketplace, however, disciplines other professional fields; doctors and lawyers who don't satisfy their clients tend to lose them. Manufacturers of defective automobiles and toasters and barbers and beauticians who provide undesirable results tend to lose their customers.

Public schools, however, are quasi-monopolies and face little competition since most parents must send their children to the neighborhood school. They face little competition and, if their operators can set their own standards, they are likely to be lax. As documented in Chapter 7, tests are subject to extensive fraud by students and educators. Chapters 8, 9, and 10 suggest that the solution to this American school dilemma is independent standards setting, testing, and reporting.

6

TESTS AS INCENTIVES

Well-designed standardized achievement tests can provide substantial benefits to students, teachers, and society. Those benefits are most likely to occur when students and educators have incentives to do their best work. Although incentives associated with learning are complex, experimental data shows that performance is optimal when students experience real consequences for doing well in school, teachers exhibit competence, and both receive personal, social, and economic benefits for their effort.[1] This chapter examines how tests can be used as part of systems that motivate students.

Testing for Grade Promotion

One way to use tests to motivate students to do their best is to make advancement to the next grade contingent on passing summative tests. This allows successful students to experience direct consequences for meeting school standards. Although such tests are rarely used for each grade promotion decision, a number of states require students to pass tests to graduate from elementary and high schools. As noted in earlier chapters, citizens and students themselves support this idea of holding students accountable for their achievement.

---

1. See E.A. Hanushek and D.W. Jorgenson, eds., *Improving America's Schools: The Role of Incentives* (Washington, DC: National Academy Press, 1996).

One bold and carefully studied innovation gave students in the Chicago Public Schools the choice of being retained in a grade or taking a six-week summer course and then passing a grade-level summative examination for promotion.[2] Independent researchers found that students who attended the course made as much as a year and a half of achievement progress in a single summer.

These amazing results were obtained after using diagnostic tests to identify students' skill deficits and then teaching directly to those areas. Frequent tests in combination with remediation efforts minimized the degree to which students are unfairly punished for scoring poorly on a single exam. At the conclusion of this targeted instruction, standards-based tests showed rapid achievement gains by most students.

The Chicago program and others like it exemplify the capacity of high standards, incentives, and tests to yield much greater progress than observed in more conventional education. At a cost of six weeks of intensive work, the students in the Chicago program saved themselves, teachers, and taxpayers a year of costly, inefficient remediation. With the help of a strong testing program, teachers met the varied needs of individual students, strengthening both personal and achievement levels.

Student Test Incentives

By helping students identify their personal strengths and aligning those strengths with activities that are valued in their respective age group, standardized tests encourage students to take some responsibility for their educational activities. Young children may need adult supervision when making decisions about when or whether to study and how seriously to

---

2. Melissa Roderick, Jenny Nagaoka, and Elaine M. Allensworth, "Is the Glass Half-full or Mostly Empty? Ending Social Promotion in Chicago" in Edward H. Haertel and Joan Herman, eds., *Uses and Misuses of Data for Educational Accountability and Improvement;* 104th yearbook for the National Society for the Study of Education, Part 2 (Malden, MA: National Society for the Study of Education, 2005), 223–259. The relations between school environments and leadership are corroborated in a report by Melissa Roderick, John Q. Easton, and Penny Bender Sebring, "The Consortium on Chicago School Research: A New Model for the Role of Research in Supporting Urban School Reform" (Chicago, IL: The Consortium on Chicago School Research at the University of Chicago Urban Education Institute, 2009), 19–20.

take learning. Many adolescents can think more independently about their long-term future. Regardless of their age, though, students need adult guidance on how to think about the value of their abilities and accomplishments. They can benefit from concrete test evidence when they are proceeding constructively toward short- and long-term goals.

Most young children enjoy seeking and receiving points, stickers, and other small rewards for accomplishments. Capitalizing on such enthusiasm, one stay-at-home mom developed a point system to reward her children and their friends for passing short comprehension tests on books they read at their leisure. Her project grew to become the now vastly expanded Accelerated Reader program, which is available in about half of the schools in the U.S.[3]

Accelerated Reader consists of a search system that helps teachers select books suited to a student's interests and reading ability, five-item tests on over 30,000 books generally available in school and community libraries, and a computer test with instant scoring. As students become stronger readers, they are encouraged to read more difficult books because points are awarded in proportion to the difficulty of the book and the number of correct answers. The program, which costs only $100 per year per student, or about 1 percent of the annual per-student cost of public schooling, maintains a detailed record of each student's progress, minimizing the amount of bookkeeping required by teachers and parents.

Accelerated Reader showed excellent results in a number of rigorous (control group) studies conducted by independent scholars.[4] The program is perhaps the best example of highly efficient computer-assisted school-level learning, of how regular feedback of results for teachers and learners (called formative assessment) yields efficient achievement results, and of

---

3. Details on the company and the program can be found at http://www.renlearn.com/ar/.

4. Keith J. Topping, and Terry D. Paul, "Computer-Assisted Assessment of Practice at Reading: A Large-Scale Survey Using Accelerated Reader Data," *Reading and Writing Quarterly*, 1999, *15*, 213–231; Stacy R. Vollans, Keith J. Topping, and Ryka M. Evans, "Computerized Self-Assessment of Reading Comprehension with the Accelerated Reader: Action Research," *Reading and Writing Quarterly*, 1999, *15*, 197–211; John A. Nunnery, Steven M. Ross, and Aaron McDonald, "A Randomized Experimental Evaluation of the Impact of Accelerated Reader/Reading Renaissance Implementation on Reading Achievement in Grades 3 to 6," *Journal of Education for Students Placed at Risk*, 2006, *11*, 1–18.

how integrating testing and rewards for achievement can accelerate learning among young children.

As children move into adolescence, their views change on what is rewarding.[5] Some sustain high levels of achievement motivation and benefit from token rewards and public recognition of their academic prowess, self-determination, and independence. For these students, tests continue to serve as incentives in showing their progress in attaining knowledge and skills.

Other students may require more tangible incentives. Motivation can build if adolescents see a connection between scoring well on tests and attaining the careers they aspire to in fields such as medicine, science, or law enforcement. Some charter schools have shown remarkable success by getting adolescents to focus on the importance of attending college and the need to meet college admission standards. John Bishop provides evidence that the chance to win scholarships to New York state colleges and universities motivates high school students to do well on the New York Regents Examination.[6]

Incentives for Advanced Accomplishments

Adolescents are often torn between wanting to belong to social groups and wanting to learn new and challenging subjects. Social groups may reward acting out, short-term thinking, and interest in cars, clothes, and dating. High school students who work harder than their classmates, especially if educators single them out for praise and recognition, can face ridicule from fellow students who would rather see academic expectations kept lower, which results in a dilemma for the many talented students.

Several kinds of incentives can be given to students who resist the antiacademic culture of their schools and take honors, foreign language, physics and calculus, Advanced Placement (AP), and other advanced

---

5. Ellen F. Potter, "The Impact of Developmental Factors on Motivating the School Achievement of Young Adolescents: Theory and Implications for Practice," *The Journal of Early Adolescence*, 1984, 4, 1–10.

6. See, for example, John H. Bishop and Ferran Mane, *Educational Reform and Disadvantaged Students: Are They Better Off or Worse Off?*, CESIFO working paper no. 1309, category 4, Labour Markets, October 2004, http://papers.ssrn.com/sol3/papers .cfm?abstract_id=615566. Technical reports for these examinations can be found at http:// www.emsc.nysed.gov/osa/reports/.

courses. Access to such courses can be made convenient and free, they can be taught in especially comfortable or high-status classrooms, and tutoring and other support activities can be supplied. Schools can support student clubs such as debate and foreign languages based on the coursework and interests of high-achieving students. Tournaments, class trips, parties, and other activities organized for high achievers can take the place of some of the school activities dominated by lower-achieving students.

AP courses and exams, sponsored by the College Board, are an excellent example of a standardized test that can serve as an incentive for advanced academic accomplishment. The courses are similar to undergraduate courses in college, and participating colleges grant credit to students who qualify. AP tests are scored on a 1-to-5 scale with 5 being the highest score and 1 the lowest. According to the College Board, "more than 90 percent of four-year colleges in the United States and colleges in more than 60 other countries give students credit, advanced placement, or both on the basis of AP exam scores."[7] Most colleges require a minimum score of 3 or 4 to receive college credit. Approximately 1 million students take more than 2 million AP exams each year.

Many students, parents, and educators are aware of AP programs and the possibility of attaining such credits. But there has been insufficient attention given to using positive AP results to shorten the college years. In principle, it would be possible to skip a year or two of college and tuition by gaining AP credit for courses and going to summer school. With ever-rising college tuition, the family savings might be considerable. States could encourage such AP policies to relieve their present budget pressures.

Another way to accelerated learning is to offer monetary incentives for high achievement. In a highly successful Texas program, the O'Donnell Foundation offered monetary incentives for taking AP courses and passing AP examinations.[8] Over a five-year period, the foundation awarded

---

7. College Board, "AP for Students and Parents," http://www.collegeboard.com/student/testing/ap/about.html. Last accessed December 7, 2010.

8. C. Kirabo Jackson, *A Stitch in Time: The Effects of a Novel Incentive-Based High School Intervention on College Outcomes*, NBER working paper no. 15722 (Washington, DC: The National Bureau of Economic Research, February 2010). Extremely large effects such as these do not require randomized field trials to establish causation just as flyswatters do not require randomized field trials to prove their efficacy. Still, further research is warranted to test the student incentive effect in other circumstances.

$100 to students and their teachers in 11 inner-city high schools in Dallas for each AP exam passed. The number of students who passed AP exams, many of them black and Hispanic and from low-income families, rose ten-fold. The schools also saw increased graduation rates for black and Hispanic students, and students who participated in AP programs attended college in greater numbers, earned higher college GPAs, and were more likely to remain in college beyond their freshman year. Similar programs corroborate these impressive results.

Some students, of course, work long, intensive hours without monetary reinforcement to please their parents or for personal satisfaction. Paying some students to do what others do from internal motivation strikes some people as being improper or unnecessary, while other critics think such projects divert attention from reforms that could have wider systemic effects on schools. But such criticism misses the mark. Not all students are blessed with parents who have the time or ability to set high goals and instill the best study habits. And even the best teachers and schools find their task more difficult if students are unmotivated to learn. Paying students for high achievement isn't a silver bullet or appropriate for all grades or all students, but it has often proven to be a valuable tool in the schools where it has been tried.

Teacher Performance Pay

With dedicated students and highly skilled teachers, it might be assumed that achievement levels will climb once aligned standards, curriculum, and testing are in place. Carefully designed incentive systems, however, may be required not only for students but also for teachers. Performance-based pay is widely practiced in private firms and used increasingly in government.[9]

Economists and behavioral psychologists have long shown that appropriate incentives, both symbolic and real, powerfully shape behavior. In the workforce, youths and adults are paid to do what others want done.

---

9. Michael Kremer, Edward Miguel, and Rebecca Thornton, "Incentives to Learn," *Review of Economics and Statistics*, 2009, *91*, 437–456; Michael J. Podgursky and Matthew G. Springer, *Teacher Performance Pay: A Review* (Nashville, TN: National Center on Performance Incentives, 2006); Edward P. Lazear and Kathryn L. Shaw, *Personnel Economics* (Cambridge, MA: National Bureau of Economic Research, 2007).

They may intrinsically enjoy their work, but they expect payment for performance. Such thinking is entering or re-entering education, including with respect to teachers. Policy-makers' interest in teacher incentives is rising, and the public supports them.

If a person seems unresponsive or indifferent to an incentive, the observer may not understand the person's perception of the incentive. The incentive may be considered small, inappropriate, or inopportune; the expenditure of time and effort for better performance may be too costly in attention, time, energy, and peer pressure. These are design problems that can be solved.

Still, nearly all public school teachers have been paid according to a "single-salary schedule" or "position-automatic system," which means that, within a district, all teachers with a given number of years of experience and education level receive identical pay. Except during the first few years of teaching, neither of these pay determinants is linked to student achievement. Even special pay for hard-to-recruit subjects such as science and mathematics and "combat pay" for teaching in difficult schools are rare. On the other hand, pay for performance is more common in private and charter schools.

Many educators and some policy analysts cite teacher performance pay for their students' learning as insufficiently demonstrated to justify further study or use in schools. Yet, the achievement failures and rising costs of public schools suggest the opposite. Since performance pay is nearly universal in other occupations and professions, the burden of proof rests with those who defend the single-salary schedule. Despite questionable claims that performance pay is unfair to educators, the present single-salary schedule is actually unfair to the millions of children in public schools who are subject to poor teaching and repeatedly failing schools. It is also unfair to unrewarded educators whose performance excels.

Incentives for results might be particularly beneficial in public schools since they are quasi-monopolies in that most children—unless they can afford private schools or move to other neighborhoods—may only attend the school assigned to them by school officials. Like other monopolies, public schools have too often been indifferent to the preferences of their customers. On the other hand, private schools more often employ performance pay; they must compete for students and produce significantly higher parent satisfaction. And many inner-city parents would send their children to private schools if they could afford the tuition.[10]

Though performance pay systems can improve achievement, they require careful design and are subject to unanticipated effects. For example, a possible design problem could involve educators who concentrate on students below the proficiency cut scores, neglecting other students. To solve this problem, the average achievement gains of all students may be taken as the performance criterion rather than simply the percentage that crosses a particular cut score.

The best incentive programs align teachers' raises and bonuses with student learning, but additional criteria may be used, such as giving the principal's assessment half the weight of the overall performance rank. Also, it would be reasonable to pay principals based on school performance to encourage them to take greater care in assessing and rewarding high-performing teachers. Making the incentive half the total compensation for both teachers and principals may be too much, but 5 percent seems too little. Given the poor performance and high costs of public schools, large incentives relative to base pay seem to be in order.

Since students' achievement at the end of an academic year is substantially predictable based on their standing at the beginning of the year, it is reasonable to gear payment to the standardized test *gains* made under the teacher in question. Admittedly, more study of teacher incentive programs is required, but the prominence of incentives in economic theory, behavioral psychology, and much of the American workforce may be sufficient evidence for expansion on a much wider scale.

The absence of incentives may be a major cause of the quarter-century failure to improve achievement in American public schools as revealed by standardized tests. The next two chapters introduce problems in the use of the tests themselves as well as promising solutions as districts, states, and nations assess their offerings, establish better programs, and initiate the tests, testing, and incentives needed to raise student achievement.

---

10. See studies described in Herbert J. Walberg, *School Choice: the Findings* (Washington, DC: Cato Institute, 2007).

7

PREVENTING TEST FRAUD

National surveys show that most students report cheating at some point during their school careers. The Internet makes one form of cheating easier since essays can be purchased and, if necessary, adapted for common high school assignments and college applications.[1] High school students in prestigious Advanced Placement and International Baccalaureate programs often indicate that pressure from parents and teachers led them to engage in academically dishonest activities.[2]

Educators make similar claims. They say the threat of federal and state legislation to close schools or replace staff encourages them to cheat.[3] Even in wealthy cities such as Fairfield, Connecticut, and Lake Forest, Illinois, principals were dismissed over cheating incidents. Perhaps the most common form of cheating is acquiring items from previous tests and teaching the answers directly to students. Cheating has become so widespread that it is now the topic of scholarly symposia, targeted intervention programs, and educational policy.[4]

---

1. The Internet also makes it feasible to detect such cheating. Written work may be submitted to Google and other specialized programs to detect duplication of previous writings.

2. Lyn Taylor, Mark Pogrebin, and Mary Dodge, "Advanced Placement—Advanced Pressures: Academic Dishonesty among Elite High School Students," *Educational Studies*, 2003, *33*, 403–421.

3. Donald Deere and Wayne Strayer, *Put Schools to the Test: School Accountability, Incentives, and Behavior*, working paper no. 0113, Department of Economics, Texas A&M University, 2001.

4. David Callahan, *The Cheating Culture: Why More Americans are Doing Wrong to Get Ahead* (New York: Harcourt, 2004).

It might be added that some educators may deliberately overlook ill-disguised student cheating since their invalid results may make it appear that they themselves are doing their jobs well. But evidence suggests that such fraud harms students.[5] Aside from the ethical and test validity issues, students may develop elevated views of their abilities gained from cheating and other shortcuts. Students' belief in ability rather than hard work undermines their success in school and in adult life. No matter how able, they will inevitably fail objective tests and life's trials, and their previously justified confidence may collapse.[6]

Student Cheating

There are multiple forms of academic dishonesty, but on tests students usually cheat in one of three ways.[7]

- They capitalize on others' weaknesses to gain a personal advantage when preparing for a test.
- They give, take, or receive information during a test in ways that violate the standardization procedures.
- They use prohibited materials during a test.

Students who cheat

Though the research on student cheating is less than rigorous, a critical summary[8] of it suggests that cheating grows with age during the school year and dissipates during the college years. Students from families of

---

5. Regina Loughran and Thomas Comiskey, *Cheating the Children: Educator Misconduct on Standardized Tests*, report of the City of New York Special Commissioner of Investigation for the New York City School District (December 1999); Carol Dweck, *Mindset: The New Psychology of Success* (New York, NY: Random House, 2006).

6. Carol Dweck, *Mindset: The New Psychology of Success* (New York, NY: Random House, 2006).

7. Gregory J. Cizek, *Cheating on Tests: How to Do It, Detect It, and Prevent It* (Hillsdale, NJ: Lawrence Erlbaum Associates, 1999).

8. Angela D. Miller, Tamera B. Murdock, Eric M. Anderman, and Amy L. Poindexter, "Who are All These Cheaters? Characteristics of Academically Dishonest Students," In Eric M. Anderman and Tamera B. Murdock, eds., *Psychology of Academic Cheating* (New York: Elsevier Academic Press, 2007), 9–32.

higher socioeconomic status are more likely than others to cheat, perhaps because they face more pressure to prepare for college and perhaps because children from poor families may envision entering the workforce soon after or before high school graduation. Similarly, students with strong academic records[9] are also more inclined to cheat. Self-identified cheaters enrolled in Advanced Placement indicated that they cheated because they feared being excluded from these prized programs if their family members, educators, and peers knew their actual abilities. Social incentives for remaining in the program were high enough that students cheated to stay enrolled.

Some working-class and poor students, who tend to see high school as more of a burden than an opportunity, report a willingness to cheat if it helps them restrict the role of schooling in their lives.[10] Some of them reported cheating because they aligned their own interests with their peer group in the school that saw cheating as socially acceptable and even valued. These views were associated with perceptions that classroom procedures were arbitrary or unfair, and because cheating seemed exciting.

Students who find schoolwork boring or too challenging are more likely to try cheating. The roots of this problem lie with the traditional school experience as a whole. For example, it is nearly impossible, especially in high school, to teach students who have radically different degrees of preparation. Most schools attempt to avoid the near impossible task of teaching calculus and consumer mathematics in the same class, and most American high schools track students into suitable courses, especially mathematics, but this is less easily done in other subjects.[11] These then are problems, not of testing but of the level of courses being ill-suited for students with varying degrees of preparation, or of schools that have a

9. Lyn Taylor, Mark Pogrebin, and Mary Dodge, "Advanced Placement—Advanced Pressures: Academic Dishonesty among Elite High School Students," *Educational Studies*, 2003, *33*, 403–421; Tamera B. Murdock, Ann S. Beauchamp, and Amber M. Hinton, "Predictors of Cheating and Cheating Attributions: Does Classroom Context Influence Cheating and Blame for Cheating?" *European Journal of Psychology of Education*, 2008, *23*, 477–492.

10. Theresa A. Thorkildsen, Courtney J. Golant, and L. Dale Richesin, "Reaping What We Sow: Cheating as a Mechanism of Moral Engagement," in Eric M. Anderman and Tamera B. Murdock, eds., *Psychology of Academic Cheating* (New York: Elsevier Academic Press, 2007), 171–202.

11. See Tom Loveless. "The Tracking and Ability Grouping Debate," *Fordham Report*, 2, 8 (August 1998), 1–27.

focus or reputation for excellence in areas that are not of interest to their students.[12]

Detecting and Deterring Student Cheating

Beginning in the early 1970s, test developers developed algorithms to detect cheating by students in their patterns of item responses. William Angoff, for example, described a number of ways to detect cheating using item difficulty and the logic that if students are able to answer difficult items, they should also be able to answer easy items.[13]

Adaptive tests, described in Chapter 4, make cheating difficult since a potential cheater is unlikely to confront the same item as students seated nearby. The large item banks often used with adaptive tests also reduce the likelihood of cheating since it may be easier to actually master the material than to memorize answers or get away with crib sheets for the many items potentially on the test.

These solutions can go a long way toward solving the cheating problem with standardized tests. In more usual teacher-prepared classroom testing, essays answers written in class help prevent cheating described in Chapter 4. Using these examinations repeatedly can help compensate for their limited validity and reliability. Though they are clearly assessments, they can be essential parts of the learning experience and the basis of reteaching.

With respect to some of the reasons students give for cheating, testing by itself may have little to contribute. Cheating on formative tests makes it more difficult for teachers to identify specific gaps in knowledge and understanding, and therefore means both the student and the teacher will have to waste time going over topics that the student already has mastered. Explaining this to students should reduce the incentive to cheat, since students value their "free" time just as highly as do adults. But this reasoning doesn't apply to AP and most other high-stakes tests.

---

12.   Herbert J. Walberg and Arthur J. Reynolds, eds., *Can Unlike Students Learn Together: Grade Retention, Tracking, and Grouping* (Greenwich, CT: Information Age Publishing, 2004).

13.   William H. Angoff, "The Development of Statistical Indices for Detecting Cheaters," *Journal of the American Statistical Association*, 1974, 69, 44–49.

Student motivation to do well and not cheat on tests can be improved by ensuring that students are taking the level of courses that is suitable to their needs and ability. Cheating out of frustration or boredom may then be reduced. Similarly, students with a strong interest in a particular subject—perhaps history or science—might do best in a school that communicates to students and the community that history or science is a particular area of excellence. Loyalty to the school then becomes a reason not to cheat on tests.

Cheating by Administrators and Teachers

Cheating among educators rose since the establishment of federal No Child Left Behind and related state legislation and the required introduction of high-stakes tests in most public schools.[14] An analysis of a large collection of news articles showed extensive cheating and what might be called "near cheating," leading to spuriously high test scores.[15] The following were among the practices reported in the review:

- Expelling students whose normal coursework suggests they would not score well on grade-level tests.
- Forcing students who might score poorly to leave the school and join alternative schools for students with special needs.
- Working with test developers to change any reports that are shared with the public.
- Narrowing the curriculum covered in the school to include only information that is likely to be on the test.
- Replacing regular mastery lessons with test preparation activities.
- Encouraging students likely to score poorly to be absent on testing days and assigning them to special education groups that are not tested.

---

14. Donald Deere and Wayne Strayer, "Putting Schools to the Test: School Accountability, Incentives, and Behavior," working paper no. 0113, Department of Economics, Texas A&M University, 2001.

15. Sharon L. Nichols and David C. Berliner, "The Pressure to Cheat in a High-Stakes Testing Environment," in Eric M. Anderman and Tamera B. Murdock, eds., *Psychology of Academic Cheating* (New York: Elsevier Academic Press, 2007), 289–311. See also David N. Figlio, "Testing, Crime, and Punishment," *Journal of Public Economics*, 2006, *90*, 837–851; Walt Haney, "The Myth of the Texas Miracle in Education," *Education Policy Analysis Archives*, 2000, *8*, 41.

Teachers have been caught giving students more time than allowed for testing, altering students' answer sheets, and removing weak answer sheets from the set to be scored.[16] The existence of more subtle forms of cheating led one scholar who observed how teachers prepare students for tests to propose a catalog of practices, including the following legitimate practices:[17]

- Offering the standard curriculum regardless of its relevance to the test.
- Teaching general test-taking strategies and skills.
- Exhorting students to do their best.
- Trying to inoculate students against any stress associated with tests.
- (perhaps borderline) Teaching students about the general content, not the specific items, known to be on the test.

Illegitimate practices include the following:

- Teaching the actual test content and items, and showing students how to answer questions.
- Using practice tests that contain items that are parallel in form to those on the test.
- Giving students answers during the test session.

Detecting Educators' Cheating

When districts adopt a new test, their test scores often appear substantially lower. With each subsequent year, however, the scores tend to rise.[18] As educators become more familiar with the content of the new test they emphasize it, and the scores rise. The scores on high-stakes tests tend to rise substantially while scores on low-stakes tests remain the same. Increases attributable to better alignment of curriculum and instruction with standards are desirable, but teaching the test content itself yields misleading

16. Sharon L. Nichols and David C. Berliner, "The Pressure to Cheat in a High-Stakes Testing Environment," in Eric M. Anderman and Tamera B. Murdock, eds., *Psychology of Academic Cheating* (New York: Elsevier Academic Press, 2007), 289–311.

17. Mary Lee Smith, "Meanings of Test Preparation," *American Educational Research Journal*, 1991, 28(3), 521–542.

18. Daniel Koretz, *Measuring Up: What Educational Testing Really Tells Us* (Cambridge, MA: Harvard University Press, 2008), 244–249.

results since the content of the test is usually only a small sample of what is intended in the standards.

In large districts, it can be especially difficult to detect cheating by educators, but Brian Jacob[19] predicted a rise in tests scores when high-stakes testing was introduced in Chicago as a means of evaluating teacher performance. Using a clever algorithm on information in 700,000 sets of student answers, and nearly 100 million responses to the items, he confirmed this prediction. He found aberrant answer sheets with many responses to easy items wrong and hard items right. He also found unrealistically increased spikes in achievement in classrooms only for the year in which their teacher was suspected of cheating. In related work[20] with Steven Levitt (co-author of the best seller *Freakonomics*), Jacob found confirming relapses to poor test scores among students formerly in classes suspected of cheating. Some of the cheating teachers were identified and removed from their jobs as a result of such statistical patterns, but the methods to remove cheating educators may be too complicated for many school districts and states to use routinely. Subsequent chapters argue that tests, testing, and publication of results by independent organizations are the best solution to such problems if the results are to be taken seriously.

Deterring Educators' Fraud

The consequences of academic dishonesty are grave. Students may get a false sense of their academic achievement, which will leave them ill-prepared for academic challenges in college or during their careers. Fraud deprives teachers of the accurate and reliable information they need to tailor their efforts to students' needs and compare their own performance to that of other teachers. Principals, administrators, and taxpayers are all denied the information they need to play their roles in managing and overseeing schools.

---

19. Brian A. Jacob, "Accountability, Incentives, and Behavior: The Impact of High-stakes Testing in the Chicago Public Schools," *Journal of Public Economics*, 2005, 89, 761–796.

20. Brian A. Jacob and Steven D. Levitt, *Catching Cheating Teachers: The Results of an Unusual Experiment in Implementing Theory*, NBER working paper no. 9414 (Washington, DC: Brookings-Wharton Papers on Urban Affairs, January 2003), 185–209.

Chastising students, teachers, or administrators about how the illegitimate practices invalidate test scores and ultimately harm them may be futile, partly because it may be in their perceived self-interest to cheat. Educating them about their "true" self-interest may also be futile so long as cheating is difficult to detect or if the consequences of being caught are not perceived as being very large. What can be done?

Experiments show that students cheat less when the risks and penalties of being caught are high.[21] This argues for increased diligence in detecting and punishing cheaters. It is reasonable to assume that educators respond to incentives the same way students do, so firing educators caught cheating and taking away their licenses would signal that cheating is being dealt with seriously.

Some studies and expert opinions suggest that the culture of cheating may be changing for the better.[22] Students, teachers, and education leaders may jointly develop an honor code and take shared responsibility for detecting cheating. These codes may call attention to the unfairness of cheating, and they may reward students and educators ceremonially for doing honorable and superior work.

Yet, policing and voluntary compliance may not deter widespread student and educator cheating on tests in K–12 schools. For this reason, Chapter 9 proposes that independent auditing organizations develop blueprints and tests aligned with standards, administer the tests, and report the results to parents, citizens, legislators, school boards, and educators. Analogous auditing has long been required of businesses to protect shareholder interest and to inform shareholders of the firms' progress.

---

21. Daniel S. Nagin and Greg Pogarsky, "An Experimental Investigation of Deterrence: Cheating, Self-Serving Bias, and Impulsivity," *Criminology*, 2003, *41*, 167–193.

22. Donald L. McCabe, Linda K. Trevino, and Kenneth D. Butterfield, "Cheating in Academic Institutions: A Decade of Research," *Ethics and Behavior*, 2001, *11*, 219–232.

8

STANDARDS AND TESTING

The role and importance of first-rate standards for learning has been a subtext of this book so far. This chapter shows how aligning curriculum, teaching, and tests with first-rate standards benefits learning but then reveals that U.S. public school standards and practices fall short. So how are first-rate standards established? What risks does the creation of *national* standards pose? And should there be a single set of national standards or competing standards? The rest of this chapter seeks to answer these questions.

Benefits of High-Quality Standards

As early as 1980, consistent studies showed the positive effects of clear, high standards in many circumstances and organizations. In 1981, the flagship journal of the American Psychological Association reported the findings by four distinguished psychologists:

> A review of both laboratory and field studies on the effects of setting goals when performing a task found that in 90 percent of the studies, specific and challenging goals lead to higher performance than easy goals, "do your best" goals, or no goals. Goals affect performance by directing attention, mobilizing effort, increasing persistence, and motivating strategy development. Goal setting is most likely to improve task performance when the goals are

specific and sufficiently challenging, the subjects have sufficient ability, feedback is provided to show progress in relation to the goal, rewards such as money are given for goal attainment, the experimenter or manager is supportive, and assigned goals are accepted by the individual.[1]

Twenty years later, a 660-page handbook compiled the powerful and pervasive evidence of the benefits of high, specific standards.[2]

Well-defined standards and aligned tests can have huge benefits. Based on well-defined subject matter standards, students may accelerate their progress by skipping material or even classes for which they already qualified. Recognized high standards and aligned examinations can facilitate, through merit-based decisions, the passage of hard-working students to advanced courses, demanding schools, and selective colleges. As a consequence, highly able students might graduate at age 16 or even younger and begin college work.

Well-formed standards can facilitate development of placement and admission examinations that ensure that entering students have mastered subjects and ideas that are prerequisite to the level of instruction they will receive at the school.[3] This addresses a major problem that teachers in the U.S. face: students who enter their classroom with widely differing levels of subject matter mastery. Such differences often force teachers to lower the content of their lessons to the competence of the slowest or least-prepared students in the classroom, which can bore high achievers. When teachers do not make such accommodations, their lessons can frustrate lower achievers, leading them to act out, cheat, or simply give up.

Standards-based exams can identify students with aptitudes, interests, and perhaps learning styles that would make them a good fit with the school's areas of specialization and excellence, such as art, science, or

---

1. Edwin A. Locke, N. Shaw, Lisa M. Saari, and Gary P. Latham, "Goal Setting and Task Performance," *Psychological Bulletin,* 90 (1981), 125–152; quote on 125.

2. Edwin A. Locke, ed., *Handbook of Principles of Organizational Behavior* (Oxford, UK: Blackwell Publishers, 2000).

3. Herbert J. Walberg and Arthur J. Reynolds, eds., *Can Unlike Students Learn Together: Grade Retention, Tracking, and Grouping* (Greenwich, CT: Information Age Publishing, 2004); Tom Loveless, "Tracking and Detracking: High Achievers in Massachusetts Middle Schools," (Washington, DC: Thomas B. Fordham Foundation, December 2009).

vocational training.[4] This helps tap students' internal motivation, create school spirit, and increase the level of student-to-student encouragement to achieve the school's stated objectives, all of which can help raise achievement levels.

The process of using tests to sort students by their interests and aptitudes can be legitimately criticized for reducing the diversity of student bodies. To the extent that differences in academic preparation and vocational interests reflect racial, religious, and gender differences—which in some areas and to some extent they probably do—they also compete with integration goals. Demographic diversity within schools does help students constructively learn about groups other than their own, which is a social good. But this potential benefit must be weighed against the cost of imposing a one-size-fits-all model of education on students with genuinely different needs and interests. Given the objectively poor levels of achievement of American students, that potential value seems highly subordinate

Aligning standards and tests also supports digital learning techniques, basically instruction delivered through Internet-based environments.[5] Computer-administered adaptive tests, described in Chapter 4, enable educators to pinpoint the knowledge and skill gaps of each student, allowing them to teach or reteach what the student needs most. The remarkable speed with which the Internet is able to process information means that integrated classroom tests can give students immediate feedback while they are still focused on an item and pondering the right answer. Standards are essential to creating the blueprints for these standardized achievement tests. They dictate the questions, stems, and distracters that appear in the Web-based item banks. If the standards are lax or underutilized, these tests and related digital learning tools will not achieve their goal of accelerating learning.

High-quality standards are partly responsible for the high academic achievement of students in Japan, Korea, and economically emerging East Asian countries, a point discussed further in the next section. Their greater

---

4. Herbert J. Walberg, *School Choice: The Findings* (Washington, DC: Cato Institute, 2007).

5. Grover J. Whitehurst, *Curriculum Then and Now*, http://www.hoover.org/taskforces/taskforces/education/AE2030.

level of learning helps to explain their countries' impressive economic growth rates, up to 10 percent a year in a recent decade, while the U.S. and Western Europe lagged at 1 to 3 percent.[6] The association of scientific literacy and economic productivity was documented nearly three decades ago and is not in dispute.[7]

Astonishing Asian growth, moreover, is not limited to the smaller countries. China and India, each with more than 1 billion people—three times the U.S. population—have averaged about 8 percent economic growth annually in the past decade. They host more than 150 R&D facilities of Fortune 500 companies. China's Huawei, a telecom giant, applied for more patents in 2008 than did any other firm that year. Thanks to cheap labor and high K–12 standards, Asian companies can manufacture cars for $3,000 each and computers for $300.[8] Chinese goods fill Wal-Mart superstores, where a pair of jeans costs as little as $7 and microwaves $29. Western "medical tourists" go to India for heart transplants for as little as one-fifth the total U.S. cost, including transportation and a leisurely recovery.

The benefits of standards, then, extend from students who receive a better quality education to teachers who find their students better-prepared to learn, to parents and policy-makers who receive tools with which to hold educators accountable for results, and finally to the entire nation by creating the productivity gains that keep a nation economically competitive in a global economy. These benefits, despite being well documented, are seldom mentioned in the national debate over school reform.

Lax School Standards in the U.S.

Along with Australia and Canada, the U.S. lacks a national curriculum and national standards. Teachers of students who have migrated from other states cannot count on what the students have been taught. Even within states, districts, and schools, students, because of lackadaisical specifica-

---

6. Erik A. Hanushek and Ludger Woessmann, *Education Quality and Economic Growth* (Washington, DC: World Bank, 2007).

7. Herbert J. Walberg, "Scientific Literacy and Economic Productivity in International Perspective," *Daedalus*, 1983, *112*, 1–28.

8. "New Masters of Management," *Economist,* April 17, 2010, 11. The rest of the price estimates in this paragraph come from this same source.

tion and enforcement of standards, usually have sharply varying degrees of mastery of knowledge and skills, which encourages the repetitive teaching of prerequisites grade after grade much more often than in countries with national curricula and standards.

Leading to further inconsistency are nationally published textbooks, tests, and other materials that cannot possibly suit different state standards and blueprints. Then, too, these various uncoordinated parts of vast congeries change independently of one another, which is attributable in part to vendors selling miscellaneous, unproven products and to state, district, and school education leaders who feel compelled to offer their reforms *du jour*.

State standards, moreover, are often low and undemanding. Paul Peterson and Frederick Hess compared the congressionally commissioned, well-regarded National Assessment of Educational Progress (NAEP) proficiency results with each state's proficiency results and found highly unfavorable state results overall.[9] Few state standards and corresponding tests fostered the achievement gains sought by the federal No Child Left Behind and related state legislation.

Comparing students in countries with rigorous national standards with U.S. students, where state standards are low and national standards do not exist, is disheartening. Key surveys include Trends in International Mathematics and Science Study (TIMSS, started in 1995), the Program for the International Student Assessment (PISA, started in 2000), Progress in International Reading Literacy Study (PIRLS, started in 2001), and Programs for the International Assessment of Adult Competencies (PIAAC, to be started in 2011).[10]

The Organisation for Economic Co-operation and Development (OECD) ranked 57 countries by their K–12 students' performance in science and mathematics.[11] As shown in the table on page 72, U.S. students

---

9. Paul E. Peterson and Frederick M. Hess, "Few States Set World-Class Standards," *Education Next*, 2008, *8*, 70–73.

10. Information on their reports can be found at http://nces.ed.gov/surveys/international/assessments.asp.

11. Stéphane Baldi, Ying Jin, Melanie Skemer, Patricia J. Green, Deborah Herget, and Holly Xie, "Highlights From PISA 2006: Performance of U.S. 15-Year-Old Students in Science and Mathematics Literacy in an International Context," report no. 2008–016 (Washington, DC: National Center for Educational Statistics, December 2007).

scored in the middle to lower level of the pack, despite our much higher level of income and much higher levels of spending per student. The achievement results are corroborated in the most recent OECD study released in 2010.[12]

2006 Analysis of How U.S. Ranked Internationally in Science and Math

Ranking of nations	Science	Math
# Scoring higher than the U.S.	22	31
# Scoring lower than the U.S.	22	20
# Scoring the same as the U.S.	12	5

These studies reveal high achievement levels in the East Asian school systems of Korea, Hong Kong, and Singapore, undoubtedly attributable in part to the national standards for schools and rigorous selection examinations for admission to various levels of education, which give parents and students a strong incentive to prepare well. Even so, Asian schools tend to have substantially greater retention rates than U.S. schools. So the high test scores are attributable to effective schools, not to high dropout rates that would leave only an elite minority to finish middle and high schools.

Many countries with national standards make the examination results available and comprehensible to attentive publics, allowing citizens and parents to compare schools, engendering competition among the schools; encouraging teachers, parents, and children in the lower grades to work hard for admission to the best universities; and making it possible to hold students accountable for their achievement. There is simply no counterpart in the U.S. to this standards-driven system of incentives for high achievement and accountability for results.

Toward Higher American Standards

In response to low standards, several pioneering authors set forth specific, high standards geared to successive, appropriate grade levels. The

---

12. Sam Dillon, "Top Test Scores From Shanghai Stun Educators," *New York Times,* December 7, 2010, http://www.nytimes.com/2010/12/07/education/07education.html.

best-selling advocate of "core knowledge" is E.D. Hirsch Jr. Hirsch's book *Cultural Literacy: What Every American Needs to Know* contains a 63-page appendix of terms and phrases. Hirsch persuasively argued that mastery of this material is necessary for participation in American society, and it should, therefore, be taught in school.[13]

On this theme, Hirsch also wrote *The Schools We Need and Why We Don't Have Them* (1996) and edited the Core Knowledge series, which specifies content for each grade level. These are highly influential works that accelerated interest in specific subjects and their sequencing across the grades. Hirsch is one of the few authors of education books that have sold more than a million copies, an indicator of widespread interest in what students should learn.

In addition to Hirsch's work, organizations of national standing have set forth subject matter standards in mathematics, science, history, social studies, language arts, foreign languages, health, technology, and other subjects. From 28 of these sets of grade-level standards, Robert Marzano assembled 7,923 terms classified by grade that can serve as candidates for a more limited set of essential ideas for students to learn. In early mathematics, for example, students should learn the meaning of "addition" and "number line." In high school English, they should learn the meanings of "acronym" and "lyric poem."

Like Hirsch, Marzano makes a detailed case for the importance of background knowledge for learning. He points out that low-income students may need specific instruction in background knowledge that middle-class students gain outside school. Hirsch, Marzano, and others made a strong case for coordinating and aligning content across the grades.[14]

---

13. E.D. Hirsch Jr., *Cultural Literacy: What Every American Needs to Know* (Boston, MA: Houghton Mifflin, 1987); *The Schools We Need and Why We Don't Have Them* (New York, NY: Doubleday, 1996); *What Your First-Grader Needs to Know* (New York, NY: Delta, 1998).

14. Robert J. Marzano, *Building Background Knowledge for Academic Achievement* (Alexandria, VA: Association for Supervision and Curriculum Development, 2004). See also William J. Bennett, Chester E. Finn Jr., and J.T.E. Cribb, *The Educated Child: A Parent's Guide from Preschool through Eighth Grade* (New York, NY: Free Press, 1999). The International Baccalaureate is a highly successful program with high, uniform standards available in many parts of the world http://www.ibo.org/.

Hurdles and Guidelines for National Standards

Perhaps national standards in the U.S., as in most other countries in the world, might help save the day. If so, they must overcome major hurdles.

In the past, interest groups inside and outside the K–12 education system asserted their views about what standards to include and how to prioritize them. Some seek to sidestep newer, results-based accountability efforts and minimize the extent to which new standards cover the range and rigor of content needed to prepare students for further education and for the workforce. Others seek to advance ideological agendas or place disproportionate emphasis on some subjects, such as English and mathematics, at the expense of other subjects, such as history and science. It remains to be seen whether standards can be agreed upon and written with the clarity, specificity, and rigor comparable to the high standards of Advanced Placement exams or the national standards of other countries.

Another concern, one that is most central to this book, is whether adequate tests can be developed to match the new standards. If the content of the standards is not communicated to teachers, and from them to students, and if the standardized tests used to assess learning are not based on the standards, then students and teachers cannot be held accountable for falling short of the level of academic achievement set forth in the standards. As emphasized repeatedly in this book, standards must create the blueprint for achievement tests if the tests are to perform their essential role in an effective education system.

There remain, moreover, the challenges of gaining the approval of state legislators, developing tests suited to each state, developing textbooks and other materials aligned with the new standards, training teachers in the new subject matter, and instituting the standards with appropriately redesigned curricula, instruction, and tests. These would be massive undertakings, especially given the decades-long failure of the state public school systems.

Chester Finn, president of the Fordham Foundation, a leading standards expert, and former chair of the National Assessment Governing

Board (of NAEP), offers a cautious, but optimistic attitude about design-ing national standards.[15] He wonders who will take responsibility for designing and managing standards and puts forward several guidelines that may be helpful in developing national standards:

- National standards must not completely displace distinctive prefer-ences of states, districts, schools, and teachers.
- The procedures for developing standards should be transparent to citizens and others.
- Standards in mathematics and English language arts should be balanced against science, history, and art.
- Subject matter and well-known experts should be included in decisions about what is important to know.
- Standards should include only specified content.[16]
- Existing tools and resources should expedite the identification of core standards while being based on strong evidence to support decisions.
- Standards should be subject to regular external review.
- Decision-making should be as efficient as possible while ensuring that standards remain rigorous.
- Standards should be aligned with systematic approaches to assess-ing students' ability to meet desirable levels of proficiency.

Common Core State Standards

Finn's guidelines are partly represented in the U.S. Department of Education-sponsored Common Core State Standards Initiative (CCSSI), the most ambitious effort of its kind in American history. The initiative has the commitment of governors and commissioners in 48 states and is

---

15. Chester E. Finn Jr., "Can We Get to National Standards, Considering the Pitfalls?" *The Education Gadfly*, 2009, 9, 1.

16. This is a modified version of the comments of Chester E. Finn Jr. in "Can We Get to National Standards, Considering the Pitfalls?" *The Education Gadfly*, 2009, 9, 1, and Chester E. Finn Jr., Liam Julian, and Michael J. Petrilli, *The State of Standards 2006* (Washington, DC: Thomas B. Fordham Foundation, August 2006). Condensations and deviations from these texts are my own. See the original for further details.

coordinated by the National Governors Association and the Council of Chief State School Officers. According to the initiative's website:

> The draft standards, developed in collaboration with teachers, school administrators, and experts, seek to provide a clear and consistent framework to prepare children for college and the workforce. The NGA Center and CCSSO have received feedback on the drafts from national organizations representing, but not limited to, teachers, postsecondary education (including community colleges), civil rights groups, English language learners, and students with disabilities.
>
> These draft standards define the knowledge and skills students should have within their K–12 education careers so that they will graduate high school able to succeed in entry-level, credit-bearing academic college courses and in workforce training programs. The standards are:
>
> - Aligned with college and work expectations;
> - Clear, understandable, and consistent;
> - Include rigorous content and application of knowledge through high-order thinking skills;
> - Build upon strengths and lessons of current state standards;
> - Informed by other top-performing countries, so that all students are prepared to succeed in the global economy and society; and
> - Based on evidence.[17]

According to several independent authorities, the initial draft of the Common Core standards compare favorably to the well-known standards of NAEP, Trends in International Mathematics and Science Study (TIMSS), and the Program for the International Student Assessment (PISA). The table on page 77 summarizes the grades given to each of the four sets of standards by scholars at the Thomas B. Fordham Foundation.[18]

---

17. Common Core State Standards Initiative, http://www.corestandards.org/.

18. The findings are from Sheila Byrd Carmichael, W. Stephen Wilson, Chester E. Finn Jr., Amber M. Winkler, and Stafford Palmieri, *Stars by Which to Navigate? Scanning National and International Education Standards in 2009* (Washington, DC: Thomas B. Fordham Foundation, October 2009).

Subject	Common Core	NAEP	TIMSS	PISA
Mathematics	B	C	A	D
Language Arts (reading, writing, listening, and speaking)	B	—	—	—
Reading	—	B	—	D
Writing	—	B	—	—

Note: The topics covered by each program were not identical.

The grades for the relatively new Common Core standards are better than could be expected compared to the others that have had a decade or more to improve. The results of a 2010 analysis of the Common Core standards, also conducted by the Fordham Foundation, are even better.[19]

Still, reviews conducted by the Pacific Research Institute[20] and the Pioneer Institute[21] found considerable fault with the standards and concluded they are inferior to those of California and Massachusetts. The Pioneer Institute Executive Director James Stergios commented, "Massachusetts has spent nearly $100 billion reforming our schools since 1993, and as a result our students lead the nation and are internationally competitive. But now we're going to ditch our nation-leading academic standards and MCAS test for weaker standards and tests because we want a one-time $250 million federal grant? It's putting short-term political gain ahead of kids." Lance Izumi of the Pacific Research Institute similarly said, "The findings of this analysis should give pause to those in California and in other high-standard states who want to rush to adopt the Common Core national standards."

19. Sheila Byrd Carmichael, W. Stephen Wilson, Gabrielle Martino, Chester E. Finn Jr., Kathleen Porter-Magee, and Amber Winkler, *Review of the Draft K–12 Common Core Standards* (Washington, DC: Thomas B. Fordham Foundation, March 2010).

20. R. James Milgram and Sandra Stotsky, "Fair to Middling: A National Standards Progress Report," white paper no. 56, Pioneer Institute and Pacific Research Institute, March 2010, http://www.pacificresearch.org/docLib/20100402_FairtoMiddling.pdf.

21. Sandra Stotsky and Ze'ev Wurman, "Common Core Standards Still Don't Make the Grade," white paper no. 65, July 2010, http://www.pioneerinstitute.org/pdf/common _core_standards.pdf.

The CCSSI quickly achieved some consensus. Yet, there is far more to do, and success depends on answering many questions, among them: Can the developers verify that the standards are sufficiently challenging? Do they align well with age-appropriate student expectations and ensure that students can learn the increasingly complex content and tasks over their school careers? Can test blueprints based on the standards be developed? Will the standards leave room and classroom time for unique knowledge and skills different states may wish to add? Can a single set of standards accommodate the huge ability differences children bring to kindergarten and growing gaps among them during their school careers? Can states with poor achievement continue their participation in the project?

The Federal Government's Role

National standards, even if developed by state consortia, go against the American traditions of local planning, control, and accountability. The U.S. educated perhaps the world's most productive workforce, an accomplishment attributable in part to the high degree of autonomy and accountability of local districts. Since that time, the states increasingly assumed a greater burden of school costs and asserted more control of education, resulting in greater spending but little corresponding achievement progress.[22]

The Common Core and national tests take this trend a dangerous (un-American?) step further in imposing federal policies on states and localities with the threat of withholding federal funds originally raised from the states' taxpayers. While the federal government will not specify the standards and neither design nor operate the testing program, it will pay for them, which is tantamount to control since it has prespecified the contractual provisions and can modify the ongoing efforts.

The federal government's record of education subsidies is an astonishing but little known failure and gives small hope that it can successfully subsidize standards and testing. It has required taxpayers to subsidize

22. Caroline M. Hoxby, "Local Property Tax-Based Funding of Public Schools," Heartland Policy Study no. 82, 1997; Herbert J. Walberg and William J. Fowler Jr., "Expenditure and Size Efficiencies of Public School Districts," Heartland Policy Study no. 22, 1988.

$1.85 trillion for programs with little effect on achievement even though the Constitution and American traditions make education a state, local, or private matter.[23] Citizens, moreover, show an extraordinary lack of confidence in Washington policy-makers. In national surveys, just 22 percent say they trust the federal government "always" or "most of the time"—the lowest figure in a half-century. Thirty percent view the federal government as a major threat to their personal freedom.[24] From 1973 to mid-2010, the percentage of Americans expressing "a great deal" or "quite a lot" of confidence in Congress declined from 42 percent to 11 percent—ranking it last among 16 institutions.[25] With ongoing wars, unprecedented indebtedness to foreign countries, poorly educated youth, the obligation of young adults to pay for Social Security and Medicare, and the high rate of unemployment and underemployment, does Washington funding and underlying leadership of school standards and testing seem wise?

In the past, lax standards or badly designed tests in one state would not affect the quality of education in the other 49 states. Putting the entire country's educational future in one or two consortia controlled by the federal government puts students' and the country's future in one basket, which given the federal government's demonstrated incompetence is nearly certain to leak if not collapse. More than cautious skepticism is in order.

The U.S. Department of Education has awarded $300 million to two consortia of 44 participating states for four years beginning October 1, 2010, to develop new tests to accompany the CCSSI.[26] Each

---

23. Cato Institute, *Downsizing the Federal Government*, http://www.downsizing government.org/.

24. Andrew Kohut, "Americans Are More Skeptical of Washington Than Ever," *Wall Street Journal*, A19, April 19, 2010. Kohut is president of the Pew Research Center and past president of the Gallup Organization.

25. Gallup Organization, "Congress Ranks Last in Confidence in Institutions," September 17, 2010. The military was ranked highest with 76 percent followed by small business, the police, the church or organized religions, the medical system, the U.S. Supreme Court, the presidency, the public schools, the criminal justice system, newspapers, televised news, organized labor, big business, and health maintenance organizations, with Congress in last place. http://www.gallup.com/poll/141512/congress-ranks-last -confidence-institutions.aspx.

26. The two groups are known as the Partnership for Assessment of Readiness for College and Careers and the Smarter Balanced Assessment Consortium. See Center for K–12 Assessment & Performance Management, "Next Generation Assessment Systems Proposed Under the Race to the Top Program," 2010, http://www.k12center.org/rsc/ pdf/15051-K12Cntr-RTTTbro-Digital.pdf.

consortia has promised to eliminate or greatly reduce the use of standard-ized multiple-choice tests presently used in all 50 states under the false assumption that such tests cannot assess "higher-order skills" and "critical thinking." As explained in Chapter 2, this assumption is contradicted by decades of research in schools and long experience in the college admission and military fields as well as in occupational licensing, which all chiefly employ multiple-choice tests. If acted on, this requirement would com-pletely undermine the usefulness and effectiveness of the Common Core standards.

The two consortia also promised to deliver tests that serve formative, summative, and end-of-course needs. This would be far more difficult if not impossible without the efficiency of multiple-choice tests. Even if it were possible, it is a mystery how 50 semi-independent state authorities and thousands of school districts can or even should achieve consensus on the specifics of content and technical features of formative tests, which usually are created and used by classroom teachers and their leaders in the course of their day-to-day practice. If such tests are administered as frequently as the consortia promise, it will also be extremely difficult to avoid cheating.

Competing Standards

It is possible to attain many if not all the benefits of national standards seen in other countries and in many industries and organizations in the U.S. without succumbing to the many problems described above. The solution is to foster the creation and use of competing standards while keeping the federal government's role in their development and use as small as possible.

Advanced Placement exams are the best example of an existing private standards system that is already nationally administered, robust, high-quality, integrated with courses (though only with AP courses offered by the College Board), and accepted for college credit at more than 90 percent of four-year colleges and universities in the U.S. In 2010 the College Board offered exams and courses on 33 topics including art history, biology, calculus, physics, psy-chology, and world history.[27]

---

27. "AP Courses and Exams," http://www.collegeboard.com/student/testing/ap/subjects.html, last accessed December 9, 2010.

The AP exams dispel the myth that standards and standardized tests narrow the range of topics or skills that teachers can be encouraged or allowed to teach. For example, the main objectives of the AP art history curriculum are to help students develop the following:

- The ability to apply fundamental art and art historical terminology.
- An appreciation for the process of making and displaying art.
- An understanding of the purpose and function of art.
- The ability to analyze works of art in context of historical evidence and interpretation, examining such issues as politics, religion, patronage, gender, and ethnicity.
- An understanding of the cross-cultural and global nature of art.
- The ability to perform higher-order thinking skills and articulate visual and art historical concepts in verbal and written forms.[28]

A second set of academic standards is the International Baccalaureate (IB) program, delivered by a private non-profit organization in Geneva, Switzerland. The program is designed to "help develop the intellectual, personal, emotional, and social skills to live, learn, and work in a rapidly globalizing world."[29] Founded in 1968, the program is used by 3,086 schools in 139 countries serving more than 881,000 students. Schools typically pay an annual fee for the curriculum, a per-pupil fee for testing services, and additional amounts for teacher training, materials, and other support services. Recognized by top universities around the world, the IB diploma requires passing rigorous examinations centered on high standards.

A third set of standards comes from New York. The Regents Examinations are tests administered to K–12 students in public, private, and charter schools in the state of New York. The tests are "aligned with the New York State Learning Standards and Core Curriculum, are consistent with state and federal mandates, are statistically and psychometrically sound, and yield valuable information that enables the state Education Department to

---

28. "Art History," http://www.collegeboard.com/student/testing/ap/sub_art.html?arthist, last accessed December 9, 2010.

29. "About the International Baccalaureate," http://www.ibo.org/general/who.cfm, last accessed December 9, 2010.

hold schools accountable for the education of all students."[30] As mentioned previously, John Bishop found that these rigorous tests yielded substantial effects on achievement of students in New York.[31]

A fourth and final set of standards comes from Massachusetts. The highly regarded Massachusetts Comprehensive Assessment System (MCAS) is a statewide standards-based testing program for public school students.[32] Students must pass the grade 10 tests in English language arts and mathematics in order to be eligible to receive a high school diploma. The tests are based on the Massachusetts Curriculum Framework learning standards, and results on the performance of individual students, schools, and districts are tabulated and released. The MCAS program is used to hold schools and districts accountable for making acceptable progress toward meeting the objectives of the No Child Left Behind Act that all students be proficient in reading and mathematics by 2014.

As reported previously, many states have their own standards. Two things make Massachusetts' standards stand out. First, the state's standards are generally recognized as being among the highest in the country and, at least on some topics, superior to what is proposed in the Common Core standards. Second, the state is considering (or may already have decided) whether to drop its own standards and adopt the Common Core standards. The state faces a financial incentive to switch to the Common Core standards since it might receive increased federal funds under the Race to the Top program.

Massachusetts could continue to administer its own exams on science and technology but would need new exams for English and mathematics. According to Sandra Stotsky, a former member of the Massachusetts Board of Education whose term expired in June 2010, "Common Core's English language standards are not as strong as the 2001 or the revised 2009 state standards."[33]

30. "Welcome to Assessment Policy, Development, and Administration," http://www.p12.nysed.gov/apda/aboutus.html, last accessed December 9, 2010.

31. John H. Bishop, "The Impact of Curriculum-based External Examinations on School Priorities and Student Learning," *International Journal of Educational Research*, 1996, vol. 23, no. 8, 653–752.

32. The following description is taken from "Massachusetts Comprehensive Assessment System Overview," http://www.doe.mass.edu/mcas/overview.html, last accessed December 9, 2010.

33. Sarah McIntosh, "Massachusetts May Adopt Weaker Common Core Standards," School Reform News, June 26, 2010.

These examples illustrate four different approaches to the design and implementation of standards. AP exams are nationwide, created and administered by a private organization, directed toward high school students, and focused on advanced achievement for college credit. Also developed by a private organization, the International Baccalaureate program serves schools around the world rather than individual students. The Regents Examinations are specific to New York, developed by a government agency, and apply to all state schools whether or not they're private or public. The Massachusetts program is similar to New York's but applies only to public schools.

The quality of all four standards is generally regarded as being very high. Sheila Byrd Carmichael and her colleagues, writing before the Common Core standards could be evaluated, gave four AP courses average grades ranging from A to C+ and four comparable International Baccalaureate courses grades ranging from A to B-.[34] The researchers attributed the success of the two programs to the inclusion of specific goals for students, teachers, and parents, and to blueprints and instructional activities closely aligned with the course standards. Students, moreover, must make sense of and draw conclusions about highly complex material from course materials that illustrate benefits to the students themselves, their families, and the communities in which they are administered. Students must form intelligent opinions and apply their knowledge in productive ways.

Competition among these academic standards is not wasteful or unnecessary. In fact, it undoubtedly has a positive effect on the persons and organizations that design and implement the standards, courses, and tests since it gives them benchmarks to which to compare their own performance. Failure by any one of these standards to capture important ideas and skills, which is inevitable, has only a limited negative effect on education nationwide because not all children are affected by the error. The existence of competing standards is, in fact, a good way such errors and omissions can be identified.

---

34. Sheila Byrd Carmichael with Lucien Ellington, Paul Gross, Carol Jargo, and Sheldon Stern, *Advanced Placement and International Baccalaureate: Do They Deserve Gold Standard?* (Washington, DC: Thomas B. Fordham Foundation, 2007).

The idea that competing private and state standards might produce better results than a single national standard may seem surprising.[35] It may be helpful to think of academic standards as being analogous to computer operating systems. Competition in that arena is pervasive and fierce, yet the results are unquestionably beneficial to consumers. Microsoft's operating systems and Office applications, for example, are prevalent among business users on computers made by different manufacturers; as such, they can easily exchange files with one another. On the other hand, Apple operating systems work only on Apple computers. Apple products are vastly appealing to young people and graphic designers, among others. Products such as iPhones, iPods, and iPads and their related applications are wildly popular.

For hard-core production programming for gigantic tasks such as airline reservations and weather forecasting, Linux is often the usual and efficient choice. Using highly skilled programming, Linux is superbly fast at crunching large sets of numbers. Competition among manufacturers and rival operating systems has been the key to the astonishing progress in computing. Insisting that everyone use only the "best" operating systems would be a catastrophic mistake, even if the one "best" system were to be chosen by a panel of the most accomplished, least biased experts.

Analogously, it can be envisioned that private firms and government agencies should compete to provide standards, blueprints, tests, and testing in mathematics, reading, and writing as well as American and world history and literature, science, history, civics, geography, and other subjects and skills. Consumers might even seek further information about the success or failure of their local schools or of other educational choices by seeking out firms that conduct school visits and analyze test results, analogous to *Consumer Reports* and J.D. Power reviews of consumer products. The next chapter describes how such a system relying more on competition and choice would work.

---

35. Nobel laureate Gary Becker and many other economists have shown how competition produces benefits in areas far removed from what might be considered traditional marketplace settings. See Gary Becker, *The Economic Approach to Human Behavior* (Chicago, IL: University of Chicago Press, 1976).

9

USING TESTS TO RAISE
STUDENT ACHIEVEMENT

Preceding chapters described principles of design, development, and administration of standardized achievement tests based on adequate, preferably high standards. The principles hold considerable promise for better understanding and substantially improving K–12 education. The education system, however, lacks some of the pieces needed to ensure that these principles are acknowledged and used. This chapter describes what an effective school system would look like. That system would have four parts: competing standards, independent achievement testing and auditing, competition among schools for students, and an embrace of digital learning technologies.

Competing Standards

The previous chapter described four high-quality academic standards systems that are operating successfully in the U.S. with generally superior results. There are others, though, of varying and often lesser quality. Competition among these standards is good for students, educators, and policy-makers, just as competition among computer operating systems benefits consumers as illustrated in the previous chapter and as in most sectors of modern society.[1]

---

1. As noted in the last chapter, Nobel laureate Gary Becker and many other economists have shown how competition produces huge benefits not only in the economy but also in areas far removed from what might be considered traditional marketplace settings. See Gary Becker, *The Economic Approach to Human Behavior* (Chicago, IL: University of Chicago Press, 1976).

Other variants can be imagined and deserve experimentation and evaluation. Some auditors, for example, might draw insight from such groups as the American Board of Internal Medicine and other boards that do not train physicians but certify their competence in various specialties while their advanced training is carried out in universities, hospitals, and elsewhere. In the school analogy envisioned here, a firm would adopt or develop standards, construct standardized tests aligned with the standards, conduct the testing programs in the schools, and report the results to various audiences.

Services provided by such firms could be funded by states, districts, and public and private schools motivated to assess their progress and to share the results with their students, the parents, and the public. Graduation from a certified high-quality program would help students gain admission to top universities and acquire desirable jobs.

The profit motive can be expected to drive competing auditing firms to set standards and develop aligned systems of standardized tests. As in the case of long-enduring for-profit rating firms such as Moody's, Fitch's, and Standard & Poor's, explicit standards and objective ratings can be expected to not only provide useful information for consumers but also help successful schools and systems prosper, whether public, private, or blended as in the case of charter schools. Soft standards and a tolerance for cheating and corruption would likely put these and other auditing firms out of business just as subjectivity, bias, and inaccuracy would severely jeopardize *Consumer Reports*.

The firms might begin with general subjects such as civics, English, history, mathematics, and science—the essential subjects for primary school. Art and music could be included with less emphasis. Middle and high school standards and audits might include advanced levels in these subjects but with more emphasis on advanced and specialized work. Auditing might be carried out in other areas of study such as Chinese, Spanish, computer programming, Web design, retail, and other specialties. Beyond the first six or eight grades, which require general mastery of the standard subjects, auditing firms might specialize in accountability and certification for the later grades. Since special assessments are required for computer programming, writing, and the performing arts, for example, firms might concentrate in these areas.

Some education providers might emphasize a speedy education for bright, diligent students who pass standards-based examinations and finish school early. Still others might concentrate on special areas of interest such as fashion design or hospitality. Others might provide a classic liberal arts education similar to the New England boarding schools that traditionally fed the Ivy League. Highly selective high schools such as the Illinois Mathematics and Science Academy[2] could build up their reputation for excellence by having their students take rigorous graduation tests.

Rigorous standards would allow comparisons of schools, including new charter and for-profit schools. Just as alums, parents, and students themselves may be proud of sports accomplishments today, they may be equally proud of good test results. Just as sports, debate, and other extracurricular activities can evoke school spirit, winning top ranks on various competitive academic standards may bring greater energy and focus on the schools' chief purpose—academic mastery. With adequate competition and objective means of measuring success, outstanding diverse schools can be expected to prosper, perhaps forming cost-efficient chains that better meet the varying needs and wants of students, firms, and the nation.

Independently Audited Standardized Tests

School boards and educators restrict and obfuscate internal information about their performance and selectively evaluate their own accomplishments in a clear conflict of interest. Scores on state-mandated tests, including high-stakes tests such as those required for graduation, tend to become inflated over only a few years as questions are dumbed down and teachers and administrators cheat or nearly cheat on the tests.[3] Since NAEP scores show no similar improvement, rising scores on state proficiency exams are spurious indicators of improvement.

---

2. See the profile of the school by *U.S. News and World Report* at http://education.usnews.rankingsandreviews.com/listings/high-schools/illinois/illinois_mathematics_and_science_academy. Last viewed December 9, 2010.

3. John Cronin, Michael Dahlin, Deborah Adkins, and G. Gage Kingsbury, *The Proficiency Illusion* (Washington, DC: Thomas B. Fordham Foundation, October 2007); Daniel Koretz, *Measuring Up: What Educational Testing Really Tells Us* (Cambridge, MA: Harvard University Press, 2008), 244–249.

Several decades of unsuccessful reforms aimed at making state-mandated tests more reliable have failed to make much of a difference, making it improbable that further efforts in a similar vein would reverse the decline of American K–12 learning and graduation rates relative to other countries. Still, the long history and success of American inventiveness give grounds for hope.

The most important change that has to take place in academic testing in America is to shift to independent organizations to evaluate and audit new and old standards, methods, test blueprints, tests, and testing practices. In some cases, such organizations may need to devise and administer the tests themselves.

Private-sector evaluators would have strong incentives to protect their reputations from even the appearance that they could be paid to inflate scores or overlook cheating. It would be analogous to a manufacturer paying *Consumer Reports* for a positive product review. Such a scandal would greatly diminish the publication's reputation and cause it to lose subscribers. Just as with traditional listed firms, public or private schools might hire auditors for independent audits and accessible public reporting. In other cases, non-operating organizations such as states and districts might fund the audits to avoid conflicts of interest.

The auditing firms mentioned earlier in this chapter are prime candidates to assume this function. In addition, others such as *Consumer Reports* and J.D. Power purchase products and services, review them, and then report their findings. For more than a century Underwriters Laboratories has been testing and certifying products for safety. The expertise of these firms should be tapped to deliver a new and objective source of information about school quality.

School Choice

More effective testing programs and publication of results would allow state and local boards to better evaluate schools and staff and, if necessary, close failing schools and replace failing principals and teachers. However, since boards have a long history of failure in remedying poor achievement, the more promising course is enabling parents and others to choose the schools their children attend. To that end, parents could study published test results to help decide what is best for their children.

Public schools faced little competition for innovation and improvement as evidenced by rising costs, sluggish response to customers, and poor outcomes—all this despite a dire warning in *A Nation at Risk* (1983) that schools' poor performance threatened America's prosperity and leadership.[4] Not only have public schools averaged poorly in achievement, but also those near the bottom and for which improvement should be the highest priority have failed to improve despite billions in federal and state dollars and many initiatives focused on them.

In a study of more than 1,000 California schools over 20 years, for example, Tom Loveless found that despite many state and local initiatives, two-thirds of the schools in the bottom fourth remained in that fourth for the two decades.[5] This and other patterns revealed in the study show that the costly innovations had little effect on the schools most in need of improvement.

As is the case of competition among businesses, an educational marketplace with little government interference seems likely to thrive if school boards and educators faced the prospect of losing students and funding if they failed to convince parents that they were meeting their children's educational needs. High standards, aligned curricula and tests, and transparent and audience-appropriate communication of test results would all be more highly valued by parents if they were free to act on the information by moving their children to better schools, without the penalty of losing the public funding that goes to the public schools where their children are currently enrolled.

The kind of choice being described here could be implemented through vouchers—certificates or scholarships good for the cost of tuition (or a specified amount) at a qualified school—or tax credits to individuals or businesses that pay or help to pay tuition for private schools.[6] Charter schools and public school choice programs also empower parents by allowing

---

4. National Commission on Excellence in Education (Washington, DC: U.S. Department of Education, 1983).

5. Tom Loveless, "The 2009 Brown Center Report on American Education: How Well Are American Students Learning?" volume 2, no. 4 (Washington, DC: The Brookings Institution, January 2010). See especially p. 21.

6. For a detailed discussion of these options, see Herbert J. Walberg and Joseph L. Bast, *Education & Capitalism: How Overcoming Our Fear of Markets and Economics Can Improve America's Schools* (Stanford, CA: Hoover Institution Press, 2003).

them to choose different schools, although the choice is much more restrained than it would be under the voucher and tax credit options.

In a free market for education, public funding would follow students to the schools they and their parents choose. Schools that fail to attract enough students would have to close, just as in other marketplaces where businesses that produce inferior products are forced to close. Like competition itself, this is not a bad thing: Failing institutions *ought to close*, since the alternative is allowing them to continue to waste resources and fail to adequately serve their customers. Consumers are hurt when businesses close only if new businesses are not present to take their place. Voucher plans, and tax credit and other school choice plans to a lesser extent, ensure that new and better schools are in plentiful supply.

The closing of public schools is so rare today that it is often viewed as a last resort or a catastrophe for students and educators. But this view, once again, is not correct. Businesses that are able to satisfy customers, such as Amazon, Apple, eBay, Starbucks, and Whole Foods, have displaced other firms on the Fortune 500 list. Of the Fortune 500 companies in 1955, only 71 remained on the list in 2010.[7] Thirteen of the top 20 dropped off the list altogether, including Chrysler and U.S. Steel. The businesses now on the list learned to compete with others for ideas, styles, lower prices, and other offerings that customers value.

Chapter 8 discussed how Microsoft was long the provider of operating systems and programs for personal computers. Now Apple, with popular products such as the iPod, iPhone, and iPad, is gaining an increasing share of the computer market. Similarly, Google's Android phones challenge iPhones. Consumers benefit from market competition because it leads to better products and services. Competition, which drives innovation and productivity, could be successfully applied to the failing American school industry. Why couldn't families make educational choices just as consumers choose computers, cell phones, and other products? If parents can choose their children's doctors, food, names, and playmates, couldn't they also choose their children's school?

---

7. See Geoff Colvin, "Long-term Thinking," *Wall Street Week*, April 22, 2004, http://www.pbs.org/wsw/opinion/geoff20040422.html.

Open Arms to Digital Learning

The Internet and advanced computer technology are transforming the education world. Educational institutions can be expected to offer computer-assisted learning programs that promise to radically improve the pace of learning for students of all ages and ability. We seem truly on the cusp of revolutionary changes.[8]

As described in Chapters 4, 5, and 6, computers have already revolutionized the design and taking of achievement tests. It is now cost- and time-effective to test more often and for a wider range of knowledge, and to quickly deliver the results to students and teachers. An example of new technology is the "classroom clickers," small devices that let teachers quiz students on lecture topics and instantly tabulate the results on a personal computer. Teachers immediately know who didn't answer and who gave a wrong answer. The result, writes education reporter Joel Mathis, is "a rolling series of high-tech pop quizzes keeping students on their toes and teachers abreast of how well their classes are learning."[9]

Public schools have been slow to respond to the technological revolution. Teachers worry that bringing technology into the classroom or (even worse) allowing students to take courses at home over Internet might reduce the demand for classroom teachers, which in fact it seems destined to do. School administrators and boards usually put personnel expenses at the top of their annual budget requests, because personnel can vote, complain, or, in some states, strike if their financial demands are not met.

Technology doesn't vote, complain, or strike when it isn't funded, and consequently schools systematically under-invest in it. The Digital Learning Council—a group of 100 education, technology, and policy leaders chaired by former Gov. Jeb Bush of Florida and former Gov. Bob Wise of West Virginia—recently launched an ambitious plan to speed the adoption of new learning technologies in American schools. "Digital learning,"

---

8.   See, for example, Terry M. Moe and John E. Chubb, *Liberating Learning: Technology, Politics, and the Future of American Education* (San Francisco, CA: Jossey-Bass, 2009) and Grover J. Whitehurst, "Curriculum Then and Now," http://www.hoover.org/taskforces/taskforces/education/AE2030.

9.   Joel Mathis, "Classroom Clickers Migrate from Lecture Halls to K–12 Schools," *School Reform News*, November 2010, p. 1.

it writes, "can also be a catalyst for transformational change in education. It is a tool that can address a myriad of challenges faced by schools, community leaders, and policy-makers."[10] The council released the following list of "10 Elements of High-Quality Digital Learning":

- Student Eligibility: All students are digital learners.
- Student Access: All students have access to high-quality digital content and online courses.
- Personalized Learning: All students can customize their education using digital content through an approved provider.
- Advancement: Students progress based on demonstrated competency.
- Content: Digital content, instructional materials, and online and blended learning courses are high quality.
- Instruction: Digital instruction and teachers are high quality.
- Providers: All students have access to multiple high-quality providers.
- Assessment and Accountability: Student learning is the metric for evaluating the quality of content and instruction.
- Funding: Funding creates incentives for performance, options, and innovation.
- Delivery: Infrastructure supports digital learning.[11]

These principles are entirely compatible with what we know about the importance of standards, testing, and accountability. If more educators nationwide get behind this effort, it could constructively and rapidly accelerate genuine school reform, achieving the kinds of academic gains that educators have talked about for decades but made so little progress toward achieving.

---

10. Jeb Bush and Bob Wise, "Digital Learning Now!" December 1, 2010.

11. "Digital Learning Now!" http://www.digitallearningnow.com/?p=91, last viewed December 9, 2010.

10

CONCLUSION

Standardized achievement tests can play a central role in improving achievement in America's K–12 schools. Properly designed, administered, and reported, they help students learn, allow educators to reliably assess the progress of students and to identify their strengths and weaknesses, and give parents and policy-makers the information they need to hold educators accountable for results.

Parents need objective standards-based test results to monitor their children's learning, help them solve their achievement problems, and intensify their pursuit of their most promising academic talents. Citizens, legislators, and school boards should demand standardized test information and become better informed about the schools' achievement progress in light of how much schools spend, what they spend it on, and the achievement effects. They need valid test information to better hold schools accountable.

Surveys show that parents, citizens, legislators, and even students favor rigorous tests and testing and want to see consequences for both achievement excellence and failure. However, many public school educators oppose the most valuable and objective type of test, the standardized multiple-choice examination. Some were turned against tests and accountability because of past encounters with poorly designed tests, and there is little point in denying that many tests, particularly those designed by amateurs, were indeed defective. They and others may be ill informed about the appropriate ways to design and administer tests and the advances that have been made in testing practices. Perhaps this book will persuade them to give tests another chance. Perhaps parents, legislators, citizens, and school boards will finally demand accountability and consequences for performance.

A few educators and administrators oppose tests because they do not want the substandard results of their work to become better known. They may refuse to admit to themselves that their teaching or management methods need improvement, or they may know it and want this fact to be hidden from parents and policy-makers. Many such educators are responsible for the cheating and fraud that has become pervasive in some school systems. Their opposition to the use of high-quality tests needs to be overcome.

Tests can be used to motivate students when they have direct consequences, such as passage to the next grade, college credit, or even cash rewards. Similarly, tests can be used to reward teachers who are successful at helping their students make progress toward state and other standards. It is not wrong or somehow insulting to teachers to suggest that they can be motivated by money to do their jobs better: All of us respond to incentives, and money is the incentive that is most likely to motivate the largest number of us and the incentive most common in most occupations and professions.

To be effective, tests need to be aligned with high-quality standards, and a considerable amount of this book has focused on the low quality of current state standards, the questionable quality and prospects of proposed national standards, and problems that arise when we ask the federal government to oversee the design and implementation of standards. Thanks to scholars such as E. D. Hirsch Jr. and institutions such as the Thomas B. Fordham Foundation, we have a good idea of what constitutes high-quality standards and the steps that need to be taken to put them into use.

The previous chapter described the missing parts that, if combined with standards-based tests, would substantially help create a high-quality education system. It is a view that is seldom offered by experts in school reform, who generally focus on just one or two of the multiple parts of the education system and therefore miss the "big picture." High-quality standards, independent auditing with tests, school choice, and unfettered use of the new digital learning technologies together would yield the high-quality education system citizens and parents want and need.

The achievement crisis afflicting America's public schools is no longer a secret. Parents, taxpayers, and policy-makers know they are spending too much for too little quality in their schools. State and national standards have made testing more prominent, and educators are increasingly being held accountable for achievement results. These recent trends are all to the benefit of education since much research shows the positive and substantial effects of high standards, standardized tests, and accountability on student learning.

ABOUT THE AUTHOR

HERBERT J. WALBERG is a Distinguished Visiting Fellow at Stanford University's Hoover Institution and a project investigator at the National Center on School Choice at Vanderbilt University. He formerly taught at Harvard University and is emeritus university scholar and professor of education and psychology at the University of Illinois at Chicago.

Holding a PhD from the University of Chicago, he has written and edited more than 65 books and has written about 350 articles on such topics as educational effectiveness and exceptional human accomplishments. Among his latest books are the "International Encyclopedia of Educational Evaluation" and "Psychology and Educational Practice."

Since joining the Hoover Institution in 2000, he wrote three books, edited another book, and wrote chapters in five other books on education policy. Elected as a fellow of five academic organizations, including the American Association for the Advancement of Science, American Psychological Association, and the Royal Statistical Society, Walberg is a founding fellow of the International Academy of Education, headquartered in Brussels. He edits for the Academy a booklet series on effective educational practices, which is distributed by the United Nations to about 4,000 educational leaders in more than 150 countries. Walberg has given invited lectures to educators and policy-makers in Australia, Belgium, China, England, France, Germany, Italy, Israel, Japan, the Netherlands, Portugal, South Africa, Sweden, Taiwan, Venezuela, and the United States.

He frequently testified before U.S. congressional committees, state legislators, and federal courts. He was a founding member of the National Assessment Governing Board, which sets policy for the National Assessment of Educational Progress (NAEP) and which was given the mission by Congress to measure the K–12 school achievement trends in the major school subjects. He chaired the Design and Assessment Committee that proposed the widely recognized standards levels of Basic, Proficient, and Advanced. Walberg was also appointed by President George W. Bush and approved by the Senate as a founding member of the National Board for Education Sciences, which oversees more than an annual $660 million on education research.

In his research, Walberg investigates factors in homes, schools, and communities that promote learning and other human accomplishments. He also employs research synthesis to summarize effects of various educational conditions and methods on learning and other outcomes, the results of which have important bearings on education policy and practice.

For the U.S. Department of Education and the National Science Foundation, he carried out comparative research in Japanese and American schools. For the U.S. Department of State and the White House, he organized a radio broadcast series and book about American education, which is distributed in 74 countries. Walberg chaired the Scientific Advisory Group for the Paris-based Organisation for Economic Co-operation and Development project on international education indicators and advised United Nations Educational, Scientific, and Cultural Organization (UNESCO) and government officials in Israel, Japan, Singapore, Sweden, and the U.K. on education research and policy.

Having served on seven non-profit boards, he currently chairs the Beck Foundation, which awards grants for children's literacy, and the Heartland Institute, a Chicago-based think tank that publishes books and six newspapers for 15,000 elected officials and others interested in policy and maintains a website with more than 25,000 policy reports from 300 organizations.

KORET TASK FORCE
ON K–12 EDUCATION

The Koret Task Force on K–12 Education is a top-rate team of education experts brought together by the Hoover Institution at Stanford University with the support of the Koret Foundation and other foundations and individuals, to work on education reform. The primary objectives of the task force are to gather, evaluate, and disseminate existing evidence in an analytical context, and analyze reform measures that will enhance the quality and productivity of K–12 education.

The Koret Task Force on K–12 Education includes some of the most highly regarded and best known education scholars in the nation. Most are professors at some of the leading universities in the country and many have served in various executive and advisory roles for federal, state, and local governments. Their combined expertise represents over 300 years of research and study in the field of education. Current members of the task force are John E. Chubb, Williamson M. Evers, Chester E. Finn Jr. (current chair), Eric A. Hanushek, Paul T. Hill, Caroline M. Hoxby, Tom Loveless, Terry M. Moe, Paul E. Peterson, Herbert J. Walberg, and Grover J. Whitehurst.

The eleven-member task force forms the centerpiece of the Hoover Institution's Initiative on American Educational Institutions and Academic Performance. In addition to producing original research, analysis, and recommendations in a growing body of work on the most important issues in American education today, task force members serve as editors, contributors, and members of the editorial board of *Education Next: A Journal of Opinion and Research,* published by the Hoover Institution. For further information, please see the task force website.

www.hoover.org/taskforces/taskforces/education

INDEX

EDUCATION NEXT BOOKS address major subjects related to efforts to reform American public education. This imprint features assessments and monographs by Hoover Institution fellows (including members of the Hoover Institution's Koret Task Force on K–12 Education), as well as those of outside experts.